Million Dollar Weekend

Million Dollar Weekend

The Surprisingly Simple Way to Launch a 7-Figure Business in 48 Hours

NOAH KAGAN
with Tahl Raz

Portfolio | Penguin

PORTFOLIO / PENGUIN
An imprint of Penguin Random House LLC
penguinrandomhouse.com

Copyright © 2024 by Noah Kagan
Penguin Random House supports copyright. Copyright fuels creativity, encourages diverse voices, promotes free speech, and creates a vibrant culture. Thank you for buying an authorized edition of this book and for complying with copyright laws by not reproducing, scanning, or distributing any part of it in any form without permission. You are supporting writers and allowing Penguin Random House to continue to publish books for every reader.

Most Portfolio books are available at a discount when purchased in quantity for sales promotions or corporate use. Special editions, which include personalized covers, excerpts, and corporate imprints, can be created when purchased in large quantities. For more information, please call (212) 572-2232 or e-mail specialmarkets@penguinrandomhouse.com. Your local bookstore can also assist with discounted bulk purchases using the Penguin Random House corporate Business-to-Business program. For assistance in locating a participating retailer, e-mail B2B@penguinrandomhouse.com.

Selfies on page 12 used by permission. Top row from left to right: photo by Tony Perrin; Gitel Hesselberg; Kailash Saravanan; Andrea Reynolds. Second row: Yann Le Bouhellec, all rights reserved frenchlevelup.com; photo by Tommy Smith; Regina Jones-Morneault, the Fabric Pharmacist; Allan Allas. Third row: Madelayne Morales R. photo by @madimoralesr; photo by Cara Boardwine; Brian Griffeth; Andrew Charles copyright © 2023 by Mindpower Growth, all rights reserved. Fourth row: photo by Ronald Annjaya; Juan Vera; Minh Duong; Mathieu Boumal.

Image on page 68 used with permission of Nick Gray; images on pages 24, 137 from the collection of the author; image on page 104 used with permission of Justin Mares; image on page 113 by Ben Kenyon; image on page 181 © copyright 2023 by Daniel Bliss.

Library of Congress Cataloging-in-Publication Data
Names: Kagan, Noah, author. | Raz, Tahl, author.
Title: Million dollar weekend : the surprisingly simple way to launch a 7-figure business in 48 hours / Noah Kagan, with Tahl Raz.
Description: New York : Portfolio/Penguin, [2024] | Includes bibliographical references.
Identifiers: LCCN 2023023688 (print) | LCCN 2023023689 (ebook) | ISBN 9780593539774 (hardcover) | ISBN 9780593716236 (international edition) | ISBN 9780593539781 (ebook)
Subjects: LCSH: New business enterprises. | Business planning. | Entrepreneurship.
Classification: LCC HD62.5 .K327 2024 (print) | LCC HD62.5 (ebook) | DDC 658.1/1—dc23/eng/20230525
LC record available at https://lccn.loc.gov/2023023688
LC ebook record available at https://lccn.loc.gov/2023023689

Printed in the United States of America
5th Printing

BOOK DESIGN BY TANYA MAIBORODA

Dedicated to everyone willing to take a chance on themselves

Contents

Frequently Made Excuses	ix
Start Here	xiii

PART 1 | START IT
Rediscover Your Creator's Courage

1. **Just Fu**ing Start** — 3
   Begin Before You Are Ready

2. **The Unlimited Upside of Asking** — 21
   Get a Gold Medal in Rejection

PART 2 | BUILD IT
Launch Your Business with the Million Dollar Weekend Process

3. **Finding Million-Dollar Ideas** — 39
   Simple Exercises to Generate Profitable Business Ideas

4. **The One-Minute Business Model** — 65
   Shape Your Idea into a Million-Dollar Opportunity

5. **The 48-Hour Money Challenge** — 85
   Validate Your Business by Getting Paid

PART 3 | GROW IT
Make Money While You Sleep

6. **Social Media Is for Growth . . .**   **109**
   Build an Audience Who Will Support You for Life

7. **. . . Email Is for Profit**   **127**
   Use Email to Make a F*&k-Ton of Money

8. **The Growth Machine**   **153**
   My Battle-Tested Growth Playbook

9. **52 Chances This Year**   **177**
   Use Systems and Routines to Design the
   Business, and Life, You Want

Start Again   **203**

Acknowledgments   **207**

Notes   **211**

Frequently Made Excuses

Welcome to a book that will help you start a million-dollar business in a weekend. We tend to think that we are never ready... but you are. The fact is, *ordinary people start profitable businesses every single day*. You don't have to be rich, brilliant, or super experienced.

But you do have excuses that have held you back in the past. Never again. Here are the ten most common and the exact chapters where we demolish them:

1. "I don't have any good ideas."

But you do have problems, and so do your friends and every other person in this world. That's all you need to generate million-dollar business ideas. After you learn the Customer First Approach in chapter 3, you'll have more business ideas than you'll know what to do with.

2. "I have too many ideas."

Choose the three you think will be the most fun to work with. In chapter 4, you'll learn how to use market research and a One-Minute Business Model to determine which of your three ideas has the most potential.

3. "Starting a business is risky. I'm nervous about quitting my job."

Risky is spending your life at a job you hate, with people you don't like, working on problems you don't care about. Don't quit your day job. Leverage the Million Dollar Weekend process (chapter 5) in the early mornings, evenings, and weekends. Once you've validated an idea, and you're pulling in enough to cover your minimum monthly expenses—aka the Freedom Number—then you can quit. I've done that twice.

4. "I've started a few different businesses. They do okay and then I lose interest."

D'oh. Any one of those businesses could have been what you wanted. Not starting and not finishing both come from a similar set of fears (covered in chapter 1). You will also learn the Law of 100 to help you push past resistance when you feel like quitting.

5. "But how will it scale?"

This phrase stops you from getting your first customer. Keep it simple and easy for yourself. Don't think about scaling, focus on starting. Then we'll discuss scaling your business in the chapters in Part 3: Grow It.

6. "I don't have enough time to create a business."

Look for the processes you can automate, or document parts of the business so you can hire someone to help. My productivity system (chapter 9) allows me to run an eight-figure business, a YouTube channel, and a blog, while working out daily, traveling, and so on. If it's a priority, we can make the time.

7. "I need to read more books, do more research, and be totally prepared before I can really start."

You will never feel 100 percent ready to start. You just need to start. Don't buy another book or watch another video until you've worked through THIS process and started your million-dollar business. I got you. Action time (chapter 1)!

8. "I'm broke as @#!*. I've spent so much money and have made zero dollars in profit."

Don't spend another dime until you've made your first dollar. The Million Dollar Weekend process (chapter 5) requires no up-front spending.

9. "I'm not good at marketing."

Marketing is easy when you have a product people want. Chapter 3 shows you step by step how to find ideas people are excited to give you money for. Then chapters 6, 7, and 8 give you the same marketing methods that I used to help Mint reach 1 million users in six months and TidyCal.com to reach 10,000 paying customers in six months.

10. "I need a technical cofounder to implement AI/VR/AR/the latest technology."

No, you need to make money first. Your customers don't want more software, they just want solutions (chapter 3). Focus on that. There are affordable ways of validating a biz without any code.

Start Here

After starting eight million-dollar businesses myself (Kickflip, Gambit, KingSumo, SendFox, Sumo, Tidycal, Monthly1K, AppSumo), I wanted to PROVE I could teach others to do the same.

In trying to share the process I realized that it consists of just a few core steps. I call these three steps the **Million Dollar Weekend process**:

1. Find a problem people are having that you can solve.
2. Craft an irresistible solution whose million-dollar-plus potential is backed by simple market research.
3. Spend NO MONEY to quickly validate whether your idea is the real deal (or not) by preselling it before you build it.

I knew I was onto something, because early on everyone who followed the process eventually launched a profitable side hustle or business.

People like Michael Osborn, who used the three steps to

turn his interest in real estate into an $83,000-a-month consulting business.

Or Jennifer Jones, who launched a $20,000-a-year side-hustle cookie business (chocolate chip for me!).

Or Daniel Reifenberger, who turned working at the Apple store into a $250,000-a-year business tutoring people in how to use technology.

The problem was, for every Michael, Jennifer, and Daniel, there were a thousand wantrepreneurs in my social media feeds who could never get started. It was a big mystery to me: If all the information you need to start a business is freely available, if the Million Dollar Weekend process works if you just commit to it, why is it SO HARD TO DO for SO MANY PEOPLE?

In 2013, I set out to solve that mystery and launched a course called "How to Make a $1000-a-Month Business." I started with a group of five beta testers—a programmer, a horse trainer, and three people with ordinary day jobs—all of whom had everything they needed to start their own business.

Two weeks after we started, I was shocked to discover the entire group practically made ZERO progress. To understand what had happened, I got everyone in a room together and did some entrepreneurial group therapy, breaking down what was holding them back.

It turns out, it wasn't a lack of skill, desire, or intelligence. The whole group was derailed by the same two fears:

1. **FEAR OF STARTING.** At some point people are told entrepreneurship is a huge risk, and you believed it. You figured more preparation, more planning, and more talking to friends would help you overcome your insecurities. But that inaction only breeds more doubt and fear. In

actuality, the best way to learn what we need to know—and become who we want to be—is by just getting started. **Small EXPERIMENTS, repeated over time, are the recipe for transformation in business, and life.**

2. **FEAR OF ASKING.** Soon after starting, the fear of rejection emerges. You have some impressive skills, an amazing product, every advantage in the world, and you'll never sell a thing *if you can't face another person and ask for what you want.* Whether you want them to buy what you're selling or help in another way, you have to be able to ask in order to get. **Once you reframe rejection as something desirable, the act of asking becomes a power all its own.**

I helped that early group and thousands since then to overcome these blocks, and if you stick with me through this book, I will help you overcome these fears and start your million dollar business.

From now on, everything you do in this book, and after, should be viewed as an experiment. This has been a profound shift for people who worry that "starting a business" is this big daunting thing. Experiments are supposed to fail. And should they fail, you just take what you've learned and try again a little bit differently.

Take me and any of the super-successful entrepreneurs and side-hustle champions I've met over the years. It's uncanny, but the one commonality nearly all of us share **is the crazy number of seemingly random things we've tried to launch**—stretching back to our childhoods. Online courses, self-published books, consulting, Airbnbs, affiliate marketing, YouTube channels, a college dating site, and many more...

And for all of us, almost all of these projects failed!

So what's the connection between all these random failures and the success we ultimately achieved? It's clearly not our expertise. No, it's because of our willingness to run small experiments.

That we eventually succeeded is a byproduct of the fact that we just try more things, period. That's what I call **Creator's Courage**. I believe everyone is born with this courage, and for those who have lost it, this book will help you rediscover the **ability to come up with ideas (starting) and have the courage to try them out (asking).**

Looking back on the early years of your life, it's easy to think of "scary" things that became not so scary as soon as you tried them. Remember the first time you tried to ride a bike? Hold your breath underwater? Climb a tree? Walk? The messiness of such trial and error may seem uncomfortable now, but the days when we weren't afraid to leap into the mud and dirty up our hands were when we learned the fastest (and had the most fun!).

Leaping is all that matters. The most courageous creators just leap more—in spite of their fear—and successful creation eventually follows. If you trace back every big company to its beginning, it all started with a leap into the unknown and a tiny little experiment:

Apple: Started as two guys who tried to build a computer kit that you can carry

Facebook: Started as a weekend project similar to Hot or Not for college students

Tesla: Started as a prototype of an electric car to convince car companies to go electric

Google: Started off as a research project

Airbnb: Started off in a weekend as a place to crash in someone's living room during conferences

Khan Academy: Started off as a set of ten-minute videos Sal Khan created for his cousins

AppSumo: Started as a way to get a deal on software I liked

> Most people never pick up the phone, most people never ask. And that's what separates, sometimes, the people that do things from the people that just dream about them. You gotta act. And you gotta be willing to fail.
>
> —Steve Jobs

Business is just a never-ending cycle of starting and trying new things, asking whether people will pay for those things, and then trying it again based on what you've learned. If you're afraid to start or ask, you can't experiment. And if you can't experiment, you can't do business.

This isn't about willpower or self-discipline. No one is going to nag, scold, or intimidate you into starting a business. My personal favorite way to approach starting a business is to have fun!

People do all kinds of scary things in the name of fun. Entrepreneurship is no exception. Make it fun and you'll overcome the fear.

So let's have some fun! Business is an amazing opportunity to learn about yourself, play with ideas, solve your own problems, help other people, and get paid all the while. Approaching it this way will free up your imagination, make you less judgy and critical of yourself, and allow you to open yourself up to the kind of playful experimentation I want you to practice.

This will be the most fun, most productive weekend you've had in years!

Why just a weekend? No time to chicken out!

I've found from thousands of students that limiting time to a weekend (which everyone has) forces you to become inventive, focuses your attention only on the things that matter, and shows you how much more you can do with limitations. You have only forty-eight hours.

Each chapter contains tried-and-tested challenges I've developed to get wantrepreneurs out of their comfort zones and into the end zone. As you follow my instructions, tackle these challenges, and overcome your fears, you'll also be growing your million-dollar business, step by step.

Here's how your Million Dollar Weekend journey is structured:

PART 1. START IT

You'll work your way through part 1 in the three to four days leading up to the weekend. These chapters will rekindle your Creator's Courage, preparing you to hit the ground running at the weekend.

In chapter 1, I'll show you how to apply the NOW, Not How mindset that's critical to experimentation. And then calculate your Freedom Number, so it's clear what you are working toward.

In chapter 2, you'll learn about Rejection Goals to help develop your Ask muscle. You'll do the life-changing Coffee Challenge that will show how fearless you are and practice the skill of asking that will empower you to build a million-dollar business.

PART 2. BUILD IT

This is it—your Million Dollar Weekend! Here, I'll walk you step by step through the Million Dollar Weekend process, where you will design, verify, and launch your MDW business.

In chapters 3, 4, and 5 (aka Friday, Saturday, and Sunday), you'll go from **Zero to $1** and land your first three customers. To get there, you will learn techniques to generate profitable business ideas, determine which ideas have million-dollar opportunities, and then take the 48-hour challenge to get your first paying customers.

I want you to work fast and stay laser-focused on going from idea to first customer. Can't get any real customers to give you money? Awesome! We'll celebrate your victorious failure (that cost little time and no money) and look to quickly validate your next idea. Remember, a weekend is all you need!

PART 3. GROW IT

What gets you to your first $1 will get you to your first $1,000. It's the leap to $100,000 and then to $1 million that requires you to create a growth machine. The most powerful growth tool today for solopreneurs is a system of content creation, audience building, and email marketing. We'll set up this system in chapters 6 and 7.

At the heart of each chapter is a challenge that delivers a concrete asset for your business. In chapter 8, that asset is the Experiment-Based Marketing approach that helped me grow Mint.com from zero to 1 million users in just *six months*. It worked so well for Mint, I now use Experiment-Based Marketing for EVERY new product, service, or company I launch.

Chapter 9 shifts the attention from the business back to

your own personal development. Now that you're an entrepreneur, you're responsible for your productivity, your training, your growth, and your time. You'll need a different approach and different system to organize your days—one that optimizes for your overall happiness above all else. (Or why do any of it, right?) This, the final chapter, is about building not just a business, but a *life* that you'll love.

CHALLENGE

Million Dollar Weekend contract.

Those people who've found success from this material do one thing: they commit to the process and they follow it exactly. I want you to be successful and create a contract, promising yourself to do the steps listed out in the book. This is your time to create your dream life. This contract will get you excited for the future and provide the necessary motivation in times of need.

Contract with Yourself

I, _____ (your name), commit to working toward my dream, having fun throughout the experience, facing my fears, and following every challenge in this book.

My dream outcome after reading *Million Dollar Weekend* is:

_____
_____
_____

Signature: _____
Date: _____

FREE MDW JOURNAL, SCRIPTS, TEMPLATES, AND MORE

If you want your very own journal to document your Million Dollar Weekend, go to **MillionDollarWeekend.com** and download the journal template.

One scribble in these notes could potentially be your million-dollar business. The most successful students use their journals to write down their progress to stay focused and absorb the ideas.

I also included templates, scripts, and video tutorials of everything in this book. You can also scan the QR Code if you don't like typing. It's absolutely free. Enjoy.

MillionDollarWeekend.com

PART 1

Start It

Rediscover Your Creator's Courage

> There are two mistakes one can make along the road to truth . . . not going all the way, and not starting.
> —Buddha

CHAPTER 1

Just Fu**ing Start

Begin Before You Are Ready

"Noah, today's your last day."

That June day in 2006 was just like any other. I woke up at the Facebook house where I lived with the other guys who worked in Mark Zuckerberg's dream world.

That morning, we all drove to the Facebook offices in Palo Alto. I sat down and began playing around with some modifications to a new feature I had helped invent called Status Updates. Suddenly the guy who'd hired me—who's now worth $500+ million—said, "Hey, let's go to the coffee shop across the street to talk about work."

It had been nine months, eight days, and about two hours since I was hired as Facebook's thirtieth employee. I was just twenty-four years old, and here I was among the smartest collection of people I'd ever been around, led by a man-child who seemed even then like he was the smartest of them all.

Ivy Leaguers. Big brains. Coders and entrepreneurial savants. All of us doing what we believed to be the most important, impactful work in the world. I got 0.1 percent of Facebook in stock, which in 2022 would have been worth about $1 billion. It was heaven.

Life moves fast. In a matter of seconds I went from living my best life ever to a feeling of deep shame and embarrassment.

Matt Cohler (early Facebook, LinkedIn, and a general partner at Benchmark) called me a liability—a word I've heard echoing in my nightmares ever since.

Most notable: While I was partying with colleagues at Coachella, I leaked Facebook's plans to expand beyond college students to a prominent tech journalist.

I was self-promoting, using my role and experiences at Facebook to throw startup gatherings at the office and write blog posts on my personal website. As the company grew from baby to behemoth, the talents that allowed me to thrive in startup chaos became, well, liabilities in the structure of a corporation.

"Is there anything I can do to stay? Anything at all," I pleaded. Matt just shook his head. In twenty minutes, it was done.

I spent the next eight months wallowing in grief on a friend's couch, dissecting every bit of what had happened. It was a defining moment. A before and after.

Part of me had expected something like this from the moment I'd been hired at Facebook, surrounded by these supernerds always talking about changing the world. It made me insecure about who I was and what I had to offer. I was not a member of the same club those guys came from, a bitter fact I'd swallowed years earlier in high school.

I was born and raised in California, grew up in San Jose. My father was an immigrant from Israel and didn't speak English, at least not well. He sold copiers, and I knew I didn't want to do that. Lugging around a copier is heavy, sweaty hard work. My mom worked the night shift at the hospital as a nurse, and she hated it. I didn't want to do that, either.

It was pure luck that I ended up going to Lynbrook High, one of the top 100 high schools in the United States. I was an average kid in a competitive Bay Area school full of the sons and daughters of America's tech elite. My best friend Marti would go on to work as a senior developer at Google; another of my best friends, Boris, was number twenty at Lyft. Other guys sold companies to Zynga for millions. Being around these people in school opened my eyes and elevated me.

But it didn't make me one of them. To get into Berkeley, I had to sneak in the side door. I got into Berkeley's spring semester doofus class (they called it *extension*), solely because another freshman dropped out and their spot opened up. Worse, during my freshman year I, a native-born American, was placed in ESL (English as a Second Language!) because I tested so poorly in English on the SAT. Honestly, I don't know how Berkeley let me in.

The early years of my career were filled with "almost successes." I got an internship with Microsoft my junior year. Normally, anyone who gets an internship with Microsoft gets a job; I was rejected because I performed poorly on interviews. Then I had a job offer at Google pre-IPO. Google rescinded my offer because I couldn't do long division. LONG DIVISION!

And then of course Mark Zuckerberg fired me.

At that point in my life, I felt like I was not worthy of success. I was not good enough. It felt like I'd already lost the game, and that everyone around me was better than me. I still struggle with those feelings at times.

And yet, even then, I knew I had something, a spark—or really, the ability to create sparks—but my gift was rough, messy, a talent that wasn't yet a skill. I had this incredible knack for choosing great opportunities, but I kept failing.

On that couch after my Facebook firing, I tossed and turned under a blanket of shame. I couldn't imagine anything worse happening to me the rest of my life. I'd been just three months away from being partially vested (don't remind me). My confidence was shot. Maybe they were right? They said I was worthless, incompetent, inferior.

They being the voices in my head.

Though I couldn't have told you this then, the best thing that emerged out of that period was a realization: I have got to figure out how to do entrepreneurship my own way and share those experiences along the way.

And so I no longer hid anything. I told everyone about my "failure." Years later, it even became a calling card. "The guy who was fired by Facebook!" And people loved it! My fears about what other people thought of me were totally overblown.

Deep down I felt liberated by my failure—not liberated to keep getting fired and lose billions of dollars, obviously. But liberated from the fear of doing things my own way; liberated to play and experiment, to find my own path.

And as a result, it lit a fire under my ass to get going on my own.

Experimenting

> Show me an experimenter, and over the long run, I'll show you a future winner.
> —Shaan Puri

And so I started again.

The next few years I tackled every business opportunity, no matter how random, that came my way—daydreaming about some big, splashy score that would redeem my self-worth and, more important, allow me to show Mark Zuckerberg what a mistake he'd made.

I was young, stupid, and reckless, but I was also learning fast—cue the montage music. I'd quickly start an online sports betting site, realize I hated sports, and then find myself suddenly traveling South America and Southeast Asia for a stretch. It was an endless experiment of launching side hustles, website ideas, and adventures in lifestyle design. I . . .

- Taught students online marketing on Jeju Island in Korea
- Consulted for startups like ScanR and SpeedDate
- Set up a startup versus venture capital dodgeball tournament series
- Blogged for my site OkDork and launched Freecallsto.com to cover the emerging internet phone call industry
- Launched peoplereminder.com, a personal CRM website
- Started Entrepreneur27.org happy hours and local events like chess meetups
- Created a conference business called CommunityNext that started pulling in $50,000 per event doing what I would have done for free—bringing together emerging business

stars, like Keith Rabois, Max Levchin, David Sacks, and Tim Ferriss

It was during this time that the variables to the Million Dollar Weekend formula came together . . . and not just for starting a business, but for creating a life that felt free and fulfilling thanks to entrepreneurship.

Each day a new experiment, a new lesson learned, living for the rush that only possibility can bring, until one day a friend showed me a product in development from an unknown company that was then called My Mint. The founder, Aaron Patzer, had created a tool to help people manage their finances, and the prototype he built blew me away. At the time I was blogging on my site OkDork about personal finance, and I immediately saw that this could be huge.

I was so excited about Mint that I told Aaron that I wanted to be his director of marketing. The only problem was, as he pointed out, that I hadn't done marketing before. So I did what I've always done—I just started. I hustled. And with no experience, I created a marketing plan that got 100,000

The original Mint.com homepage

registered users before the site even launched and 1 million users six months later—which got me a full-time offer: 1 percent of the company and a $100,000 job.

Marketing is easy when you have a great product. Mint's product was so good that less than two years after it started, Intuit bought it for $170 million. There was, however, no $1.7 million payday for me (¯_(ツ)_/¯). It was the math that sent me packing. I had figured that the company would sell for $200 million at most, which would cap my 1 percent share at $2 million pretax. Question was, could I make close to that over the four years it would take for the stock to vest? Could I create more money, joy, and insight than I could by clocking four years in middle management?

I bet YES.

I believed I could because while I was working at Mint, I was also creating the formula for starting businesses that you're going to learn in this book. I spent my mornings, lunch breaks, nights, and weekends creating Kickflip, a company that developed apps for Facebook, which then morphed into Gambit, a payment system for social games.

In less than two years, Gambit was generating more than $15 million in revenue. The value plunged later because of another guy who keeps appearing in this story—thanks, Mark Zuckerberg!—more on that later. My bet had been right: Using the principles that would evolve into the Million Dollar Weekend process—always staying alert to problems as opportunities, always starting experiments to find solutions and always asking for the sale.

I was beginning to see that to live well as an entrepreneur, I just needed to stop thinking so much and go get busy. **That meant starting small, starting fast, and not worrying about what I didn't know.**

I became an expert at *taking leaps*. Being unafraid to start new things meant that, unlike most people, I was constantly conducting experiments in my personal and professional lives, in both big and small ways. New industries. New hobbies. New technologies. New roles. New people. New side hustles. That's where I found my superpower, which taught me a lesson I want to pass on to you: **focus above all else on being a starter, an experimenter, a learner.**

> **PRO TIP:** Don't base your happiness or your self-worth on being the smartest, the most successful, the richest. Being so focused on the end results sets you up for a major fall because there's ALWAYS going to be someone who's smarter, more successful, or richer—and every time you see that you've fallen short, it will eat away at your motivation. Defining yourself by the things you do each day (the process) will get you to where you want to be quicker and more joyfully than measuring yourself against others.

That's the wonderful thing about experimentation—every experiment has within it the potential of unforeseen rewards that can change your life.

But first you've got to start.

CHALLENGE

The Dollar Challenge.

Ask someone you know for a dollar investment in you and your future business—one measly dollar!
This is YOUR spark. Once you do this, you realize the

power of starting and the simplicity of business: starting, asking, iterating. I've seen thousands of lives changed by this simple and powerful exercise.

Tell them in exchange, they'll get regular updates and a front-row seat to the process of building a business from scratch, warts and all—like a member of your personal board of directors. Sure, it's an insignificant amount, yet jumping right in and asking for it—from family, friends, colleagues—is an oh-shit starting-and-asking experience that will get your heart racing.

This is the script I've seen work best:

Hey [first name]

I'm reading this book *Million Dollar Weekend* and they told me I need to get $1 from someone.

You're the first person I thought of, and it would mean a lot to have your support.

Can you send me $1 right now?

[your name]

Oh no, I'm on the hook for this, you'll think. Good! Feel that fear and do it anyway. As my guy Ralph Waldo Emerson likes to say: "Do the thing you fear, and the death of fear is certain."

Every day, people in my audience post pictures of their first dollar with pride. It's a symbolic game-changer for anyone who's been sitting on the sidelines wishing they had their own business. And while you're at it, ask me, too! Here's my venmo/cash app @noahkagan or paypal@okdork.com. I may even say yes.

Post and tag me @noahkagan, #thedollarchallenge. I may repost you.

People like you who've done the dollar challenge

The Magic of NOW, Not How

Starting. Experimenting. Really? That's a superpower?

If you buy all the hype about Silicon Valley, everyone wears Patagonia jackets, can code with just one hand, and are all geniuses. I didn't get the coding skills or business genius part, but:

- I can start a lot of stuff without overthinking it.
- I can eat a crazy number of tacos.

Oy vey.

It seemed downright unfair for the longest time. But as I got older and started to experience some success, all sorts of people began seeking me out for advice on this thing I did, which never occurred to me as being a thing at all.

Of course they didn't come to me to ask about starting, or at least not knowingly. The people who came always talked about their dreams of running a business, about hating their job or wanting freedom or feeling trapped. The problem in nearly every instance was the same: they hadn't started.

Only now do I understand what a problem that is, and how life-changing it can be to get someone to fully embrace what I call the **NOW, Not How Habit.**

Why life-changing?

When most people decide they want to start a business, their first intuition is to learn more—read a book, take a course, seek out advice—and then take action after having carefully considered all the facts.

After all, there are a ton of top-rated MBA programs, $10 Udemy courses, free YouTube videos, and entrepreneurship how-to books—so why wouldn't you learn all you could?

That's got to be a whole lot safer, and it probably makes you a lot less likely to fail, right?

Wrong.

Overthinking seems like the "smart" way to launch, but it's far less effective. Super-successful people do the opposite—they take action first, get real feedback, and learn from that, which is a million times more valuable than any book or course. And quicker!

- **Most people:** Overthink first, act later.
- **Every successful entrepreneur:** Act first, figure it out later.

Any analysis ahead of action is purely speculation. You really do not understand something until you've done it. Rather than trying to plan your way into the confidence to act, just start acting.

So how do you instill this habit if it doesn't come naturally? Use the motto **NOW, Not How.**

> **PRO TIP:** Next time you are overthinking and not taking action, tell yourself to prioritize taking action NOW and don't worry about the HOW. After you do this ONCE, you quickly get momentum and it becomes easier and more natural.

Every moment of every day, I push myself—and everyone around me—to live up to NOW, Not How. When I want to achieve something, and there's a version I can do in minutes, I just do it. Here's an example:

Recently an ad agency was pitching our AppSumo team on a new Facebook advertising campaign. My NOW, Not How thought was followed by the dreaded promise of an email recap of everything we'd have to get started (stuff like passwords, adding the agency to our Facebook account, new content needed, and so on). "No, no, let's do all of that right now," I said, which took five minutes, saving us twenty-four hours of waiting.

I know your inner negotiator may be saying, "That sounds great, but MY idea needs more time." Stop! Power comes when you automatically implement NOW, Not How in everything you do. So no more negotiating with yourself. You're just a doer. Say it to yourself: **NOW, Not How.**

CHALLENGE

NOW, Not How Challenge.

Ask one person you respect for a business idea.

This is a quick way to get a business idea. You're going to do it for yourself and realize the power of starting NOW.

You'll realize by acting in the moment, you feel great about yourself and build momentum toward your dream life.

I'm even going to provide a script, to cut off your inner skeptic. This won't even take you two minutes. But it will create your first spark. And your second and third . . . So type this up in email—no, better yet, because it's faster, use text—and send it to one of your friends. NOW!

Hey [first name], I'm trying to come up with some business ideas right now.

You know me well, so I was wondering what kind of business you think I'd be good at?

[your name]

**Don't be afraid
to act. Be afraid
of living a life
that seems more
like a résumé
than an adventure.**

Don't be afraid to act. Be afraid of living a life that seems more like a résumé than an adventure.

And I promise, starting new things and following your fear makes life seem magical. You thought this was just about building a big beautiful business? Sure, it's about that, too, but it's also about using entrepreneurship as a way to renew and reinvent your life.

The Freedom Number Will Set You Free

I've found a simple mission to hit a monthly revenue number is the most effective form of early motivation.

I've never harbored any change-the-world/become-a-megabillionaire dreams. No big hairy audacious goals (which sounds gross anyway). My dreams were of freedom.

To make that dream come true, you first need to choose your Freedom Number.

From my eighteenth birthday until I turned thirty, my monthly Freedom Number was $3,000. Why $3,000? Because adding up what I paid for rent, the cost of the tacos and steak and wine I liked to eat and drink, and the plane tickets that would let me work from Argentina or Korea or Thailand, all together that came to a little less than $3,000 a month. At the time, that's what my living expenses were. Roughly speaking: $1,000 for housing, $1,000 for food and travel, $1,000 for savings and investment.

MY FREEDOM NUMBER: $3,000

Activities	Amount
Housing	$1,000
Food and travel	$1,000
Savings and investment	$1,000
Total (Freedom Number)	$3,000

I calculated I could work from wherever with people I love for a long period of time on $3,000 a month—without ever having to do a single thing I didn't want. For $3,000 a month, I could have my freedom.

For a long time I kept my number quiet, thinking it was an odd, silly little trick I played on myself in my twenties to make me feel better about having accomplished so little. But the first time I mentioned it some years ago to a successful entrepreneur I was talking with, they blurted out, "Holy shit! No way—my number was $1,500!"

It turns out many of the entrepreneurs I know used the same trick at some point. For some, it's a smaller number like $100 meaning they've earned extra income for a nice meal and feel a sense of empowerment. For others, where the cost of freedom might mean alimony or a mortgage, the Freedom Number is higher. For all of us, remarkably, our Freedom Number distills the story we tell ourselves of why and how we succeed into a simple clarifying goal.

Why is this tiny trick—setting one recurring monthly revenue figure—so effective?

First, it's doable. I didn't know it then, but my idea of the **Freedom Number** hit on the precisely right ingredients for motivating a serial starter. My number was 100 percent attainable, and the value I attached to reaching it—freedom!—was infinite, a relationship that was so motivating to me it always gave me confidence and served as an anchor in times of uncertainty.

Second, it's concrete and it's urgent. Three thousand dollars is not some kind of "$20 million in net worth by age forty" dream that you can put off for tomorrow. It's a monthly number you can work on today. Even better, it can be super low. You could say, "I want to keep my day job for now, but I want to make $500 a month on my own." That's just as valid. My side hustles were all small numbers, but they served as vital practice that trained the spark-making muscles that let me eventually leave the job behind.

Finally, my goal had a very specific number attached. And that focuses your mind on what matters in business, which are the things most likely to bring you customers. **Many struggle to make their first dollar because they are so focused on how to make their first million.** Focusing on an attainable Freedom Number—even better, just dollar number one—will change the way you think: What can YOU do in your business to make money this week? Today? *Right now?*

You may not need a grand purpose to start (though if you have one, awesome!), but it's also true that **if you commit to nothing, you'll be distracted by everything**. The Freedom Number helps us not get lost in abstraction or complexity; it reminds us the mechanics of business are simple.

> ## CHALLENGE
>
> ### Choosing your Freedom Number.
>
> Start by choosing a short-term monthly revenue goal—your Freedom Number—and make it a number that doesn't scare you. **Write it down in your journal and here in this book, right next to these words.**
> **My Freedom Number is:**
>
> _____
>
> This chapter can be summarized in one sentence: *Successful people just start.*
>
> I promise you: Who you are, what you have, and what you know right now are more than enough to get going.

CHAPTER 2

The Unlimited Upside of Asking

Get a Gold Medal in Rejection

As my dad and I entered the tenth local shop that afternoon, I felt my muscles go tight with a full body cringe. He'd just asked to speak to the manager in an Israeli accent as thick as hummus. Sounding identical to Arnold Schwarzenegger.

"I don't get it." His voice boomed enthusiastically after he was introduced to the store's boss. "You live in greatest country in world, and you have greatest business in sector, but you still have a crappy copier. Why? I must help you. Here, I gave much better, let me show!"

His pitch would be met with a rejection. And then another rejection. Countless rejections. Rinse and repeat. Every. Damn. Day.

But then, invariably, inevitably, a hard-won success.

This particular day was glorious, though. Absolutely glorious. He sold *two* copiers in one day! So Dad said let's go celebrate and grab some burritos!

"Why you look so sad, Noah?" he said as we sat down to eat.

Although I should have been riding on the adrenaline of my dad's glorious day, something felt wrong. Despite his ultimate success, the process of getting there felt demoralizing and pointless.

I shook my head. "So many noes. No, no, no, no. All day. Doesn't it make you want to quit?" I asked.

My dad replied with something that would change my life:

"Love rejections! Collect them like treasure! Set rejection goals. I shoot for a hundred rejections each week, because if you work that hard to get so many noes, my little Noah'le, in them you will find a few yeses, too." Maybe that's why he named me NO-ah, to remind me of this daily to keep going.

Love rejections?! **Set rejection *goals*?!**

My dad reframed rejection as something desirable—so you feel good when you get it. He was saying aim for rejection! It was suddenly clear to me why my dad was never afraid to ask anyone anything—and why he pushed for a hundred rejections a week: the upside of asking is unlimited and the downside is minimal.

And he was right!

"What's the worst that can happen?" he'd say whenever I cringed at someone turning him down. "So they said no. Who cares! And the upside of making sales is unlimited."

Asking isn't so scary if it's leading you toward where you want to go. The ultimate sales hack, the one that lets you live your dreams, has nothing to do with finding the perfect way to ask. The act of asking is a power all its own. Case in point: Kyle MacDonald turned a red paper clip into a HOUSE with a series of just fourteen asks!

At that moment when it all clicked, I sort of felt like my dad was a genius. Here was this guy with no MBA, no sales training, no self-help books, no command of the English language—an immigrant with nothing—but always a large wad of cash in his pocket. Put him anywhere and give him a week, and he'd figure it out.

How did my dad, who would ultimately lose everything to drug addiction, do it? The secret to my father's mastery of selling in a language he barely spoke is one word: chutzpah. It's the Yiddish word for moxie, nerve, audacity; it's a determined, give-no-f*cks approach to life. When Israelis say you have chutzpah, they mean you know what you want and go for it. They mean you have endless tenacity. They mean you'll do what it takes.

My mom knew this all too well. She always told me, "The squeaky wheel gets the grease," and let's just say she taught me how to *squeak*. I mean, this is a woman who tried to return her wedding-present silverware thirty years later, just to see if she could. She knew a little something about chutzpah herself.

That skill—having the chutzpah to ask for what you want, despite the fear—is the entrepreneur's ultimate and most necessary quality. **The thing is, most people don't ask for what they want. They wish for it, they make "suggestions" and drop hints, they hope. But the simple fact of business is that only by asking do you receive what you want. No ASK? No GET. That applies to every part of life. Seriously, every part.**

Having this ability to ask is the reason so many immigrants or children of immigrants fare well in business. Like my father, they aren't worried about the social consequences of doing something they aren't supposed to do because they don't *know* what they're not supposed to do. That means they can be naive and ask for anything, which is a business superpower.

You can't truly understand that power until you use it for yourself—something I was lucky enough to experience in the fourth grade, just a few months after my father's life-changing advice. I came across one of those magazine catalogs that sent kids door to door selling discounted subscriptions, like $8 for a year of *Popular Mechanics*.

I saw that the company offered a pizza party for the kid who sold the most magazines. Now my ears were open. As a chunky kid, I *loved* pizza. So I hit the streets.

I went door to door around San Jose in my JNCO baggy shorts, with a highly irresistible offer to buy magazines. I would point them to the magazines I liked best and ask them to buy one.

I got rejected a lot, but you know what? One after another said yes!

The success was intoxicating for fourth-grade Noah. My grades were mediocre, and I wasn't great at sports, but I won the Magazine Pizza Party Challenge by a blowout.

Yay, pizzzzzzzza

Getting money is not a matter of literally getting it. It's a matter of RECEIVING IT, which can happen only after one asks for it.

From that point forward I became an asking machine, and it's the thing that's produced more of my success than anything else. That's why, in this chapter, you're going to learn to stare down the fear of rejection that keeps most people from developing that ever-crucial Ask muscle.

Develop Your Ask Muscle

Embracing risk, fear, and rejection gives you the power to transform your life. It's just that simple. I've helped 10,000+ people via my Monthly1K business course, and the number one thing that held people back from business success was NOT a lack of strategy... but *Ask Avoidance*.

Getting money is not a matter of literally getting it. It's a matter of RECEIVING IT, which can happen only after one asks for it.

The illusion of eventual pain that you associate with taking that risk—what if you're judged or look foolish or it doesn't work?—is a straitjacket on your potential. Removing the jacket—stepping forward into the uncertainty with that first ASK—is the game-changing skill that starts your million-dollar business and redesigns your life.

Let me say it again, because it's that important: intentionally developing your Ask muscle is a REQUIREMENT for entrepreneurial success. The question, of course, is how you do it.

Now, I'm not superhuman. I know you're thinking: *Noah must be fearless in the face of rejection*. But no, I get scared every single time I face rejection, and I get sad when it happens. Every day, I feel the sting of rejection. And because of that, I succeed.

Just a few months ago, I was trying to hire a designer. I

was cold-emailing people—and this is no joke—six to eight hours a day. This is basically getting rejected all day long. It feels like being trapped in a bar where every woman I approach laughs in my face and walks off.

One email I got from an amazing designer I was trying to hire was so harsh I wanted to cry: "Ha Ha Ha. You really think I would leave Google for your shitty company?!?"

That. Hurt. And it always will.

So how do I get through the fear and the sadness?

For one thing—and I do this often—I remind myself I'm going to die eventually and none of this really matters. Seriously. And on top of that, would any of these people come to my funeral? No! Which is a pretty effective way to lessen the impact their rejection has on my emotions.

Then I remind myself of **Rejection Goals**: "This is going to suck. Let me aim to get at least twenty-five rejections." That alone helps me accept that I will get rejected and turn it more into a game versus a blow to my self-worth. I've trained myself to associate anything hard with growth, playing the same little reframing trick my father used on rejection.

And it's not just my father that set me up for success in this way. When she was growing up, the father of Spanx founder Sara Blakely would ask her and her brother nightly: "What did you guys fail at this week?"

It was this early conditioning to embrace failure that, Blakely says, helped her persist through seven years of almost daily humiliation selling fax machines door to door, persist after nearly every hosiery factory in America declined to manufacture her first product, and finally persist through a seemingly endless litany of noes before finally convincing a Dallas-based Neiman Marcus buyer on a cold call to put her body-shaping panty hose in a handful of stores.

The average person faces one rejection and gives up. Blakely didn't, and at age forty-one became the youngest self-made female billionaire in the United States.

Now that's a rejection résumé my father would appreciate. Remember, you could be eleven noes away from making your first million, but if you stop at the tenth rejection, you will have failed.

The trick is to desensitize yourself to the pain by repeatedly exposing yourself to it. Embrace the discomfort—actively seeking it out—and use it as your compass.

Always Be Asking

Who is the type of person that starts a million-dollar business?

- The type of person who asks for what they want.
- If you want a new job at a new company, you have to ASK for it.
- If you want more money from your boss, you have to ASK for the raise.
- If you are selling something, you have to ASK the customer to buy it.
- Even at home, if you want your spouse or kids to treat you better, you have to ASK them.

Everything that signifies a growing, profitable, and fulfilling venture—a supportive network, flourishing sales, engaged employees, a healthy balance of work and play, and so forth—all requires a willingness to ASK over and over again.

So let's get started with a few tips:

> **PRO TIP: Be persistent.** I want you to believe that almost every no you get can eventually become a yes. Persistence will reveal that most noes are actually a "not now."

My dream when I was in high school was to work at Microsoft. I wanted that more than anything. And so during my junior year at UC Berkeley, I found a recruiter on campus looking for developers, and I said to her, "I'm not an engineer, but I'm in business. Is there any type of internship I could do to work at Microsoft for the summer?"

She said there wasn't, but I followed up with her and kept asking. Squeak. Squeak. Squeak. And after the twelfth follow-up, she gave in: "Actually, we have an internship for businesspeople." I don't know if it was created for me or not, but I like to think it was. It did lead to a fun lunch at Bill Gates's house, a story for another time.

> **PRO TIP: Follow Up! Follow Up! Follow Up!** Studies show that if you initially get a no, your follow-up ask is TWICE as likely to get a yes.

At AppSumo.com, almost 50 percent of our sales come from our follow-up emails. Think about that. What a great example that follow-ups are as powerful as your first touch point. Follow up on the things you really want. I use followup.cc for email and Siri very often to remember follow-ups. You can also use the Snooze feature in Google or just write it down!

> **PRO TIP: Selling is helping.** If you believe your product or service improves the lives of your customers, sales is

> just education. You're helping people out. Reframing selling/asking as helping makes it exciting to offer your consulting or window-washing services or provide someone with delicious cookies. Once you accept that truth, asking becomes loads easier and feels much more like a communal gift than a selfish desire.

> If you believe your product or service can fulfill a true need, it's your moral obligation to sell it.
> —Zig Ziglar

At UC Berkeley, I created a consulting company—HFG Consulting—for local businesses on how they could market to college students. I saw a problem where many freshmen didn't have internships—so they would jump at the chance to work for me—and many local companies were struggling at marketing to college students.

We grew to a small army of twenty people doing this consulting. Then one day my intern Kenny suggested we do a student discount card.

My first thought was, well, *Really?* That's because there are five cliché student businesses: selling student discount cards, credit cards, T-shirts, tutoring, and something with booze. Discount cards are what business college kids often try—and fail at.

Conventional wisdom said don't bother trying, and most people would have just accepted that reality, but growing up with my crazy salesman dad had taught me never to take conventional wisdom at face value. My dad taught me to always test things out for myself.

Basically, I figured it wouldn't cost me a penny or much time to see whether local businesses would be interested, so right then and there I told Kenny, "Come on, let's go to town and ask a few shopkeepers if they'd be willing to participate and offer discounts."

Kenny paused. "You mean, like, right now? Just walk the streets and ask whoever we find?"

In my head a thought balloon popped up: "NOW, Not How!"

"Yes, NOW!" I responded.

We went business to business and basically said, "This is going to get your name in front of hundreds if not thousands of students." We just talked about how it would help them.

As it turns out, local businesses are always happy to get more customers for free, and pretty soon we had about twenty businesses signed up; enough, we hoped, to entice students to pony up $10 for the cards (which cost us 50 cents to print).

We found that giving the discount cards to student groups and fraternities as fundraising tools was our best method to sell them. We helped others make money and split the proceeds from the $10 cards fifty-fifty. Again, we just had to educate people about how it helped them.

Pretty soon, we expanded to multiple campuses—wash, rinse, repeat—and generated $50,000 within a year. Not bad for some freshmen interns, right?

Now it's your turn.

CHALLENGE

The Coffee Challenge.

Go to any coffee shop or anyplace in person. Make a simple purchase and ask for 10 percent off. Don't say anything else. The whole point is for you to feel uncomfortable. Commit to doing this today.

> Every single person who completes this challenge always posts how beneficial it is for their lives. I want that to be the same for you.

You'd think asking for a discount on your cup of coffee is no big deal, but for those that have done it and gone on to discuss its surprising power in countless podcast hours and blog posts and Twitter threads, its impact is undeniable. "This will be a piece of cake," said my brother Seth as we walked into the Panera Bread bakery.

"I'd like a club sandwich and a water," he said, and then . . .

"Uh, miss. Excuse me . . . can . . . I . . . get . . . 10 percent off this order?" Seth asked.

The room went silent. Cue the spotlight on my brother and the cashier.

"I don't think we can do that, sorry," she said.

"Okay, thanks," said Seth.

And then we proceeded to take our food to the table.

The SHOCKING part was that my brother thought it'd be so EASY, but more important, he did it and felt proud of himself afterwards.

This is the most powerful tool I've ever seen for improving your Ask muscle, and over ten thousand people have done it.

Here's an exact script you can use:

YOU: Hi, how's it going?

THEM: Great, what would you like?

YOU: I'd like a skinny low-fat vanilla latte [my fav drink, or substitute your own].

THEM: Sure. That'll be $3.50.

YOU: Can I get 10 percent off? [This is key: Make the statement clear, with a smile, and don't say anything afterwards.]

THEM: What's this for?

YOU: I'm taking a business course and this is one of the assignments. :)

A lot of you will try to make an excuse to avoid engaging with this challenge. "Oh, that's just too basic, I don't want to be that guy." "I don't want to put the barista in an awkward position." "I've already done sales for five years."

That's the whole point of this challenge: to practice *Ask*ing (and getting rejected) rather than talking yourself out of it. The worst-case scenario is really trivial. The barista says no and gives you a weird look? The people behind you roll their eyes? It's just a little bit of discomfort, but the upside is you feel strong about yourself and realize how much more capable you are than you realized!

Here are a few people and their results after completing the Coffee Challenge:

- Dieter S.: "I felt a lot more confident facing rejection, and it empowered me to successfully ask for sponsorship money on my bike-riding side hustle."
- Jennifer Jones: "It was scary, and I was not looking forward to it. But I did it and grew. Honestly, I'm insanely shy! So having to do things out of my comfort zone has helped me in all areas of my life and has made me a better person overall."
- Jason Blake: "Not only did I learn that rejection doesn't end your life, but I also learned to enjoy being outside my comfort zone."

Just do it! No overthinking; just action. Ask for 10 percent off your coffee. As I've seen in those that have done it, getting that hit of **Creator's Courage** will help you hit your rejection goals and unlock asking's unlimited upside.

Asking is a muscle, and this challenge is the gym. Learning to ask is just like building any new habit. Start small and increase slowly. The best way to overcome your fear in the long term is with short-term games of rejection.

Remember: This challenge is designed for you to get rejected! The point is to experience failure and get past it. Once you start getting a few rejections, you'll realize it's not as bad as you think. This is a powerful step in you creating your million-dollar business.

Enjoy the fear. *Ask!*

I just told you about the importance of asking. Well...

To get my book into the hands of the people who need it most, I need your help.

If my book has been helpful, can you take thirty seconds right now and leave a short review?

Think back to why you decided to pick up this book and give it a chance. Maybe it's because a five-star review on Amazon or Goodreads caught your eye. Leave a review and give someone else the opportunity to start their Million Dollar Weekend.

Before I started writing this book, I met Matt, who works security at the Austin airport. He has the same dream as you, to create a business so he can change his life, but he may never hear about this book.

Your review means the world to me AND it could *change* the world of someone else, like Matt.

Feel good about yourself knowing your brief review can change someone's life forever.

The review costs you no money (my favorite price) and only takes thirty seconds.

You can go to the book's page on the Amazon app or desktop site, or wherever you bought it, and leave a review there. On Kindle or an e-reader, scroll to the last page of the book. On Audible, go to your library page and click Write a Review.

BTW: I read every single review. And when your review happens, an alarm goes off in my office, my mom tells me about it, and our entire team celebrates like we just won the Super Bowl.

Now back to *your* Million Dollar Weekend.

—Love you forever,
Noah

PART 2

Build It

Launch Your Business with the Million Dollar Weekend Process

IN THE FIRST TWO CHAPTERS WE COVERED THE two foundational habits that will become your entrepreneurial ignition: the endless cycle of starting, and the unlimited upside of asking.

Now it's Friday, and your Million Dollar Weekend is about to begin. In these next three chapters—over the next forty-eight hours—you'll execute the simple but effective three-step Million Dollar Weekend process for entrepreneurial experimentation that will be the engine to create your dream business:

- **Finding Million-Dollar Ideas.** How to find profitable business ideas

- **The One-Minute Business Model.** How to see if those opportunities can be $1 million businesses (and beyond)
- **The 48-Hour Money Challenge.** How to test those opportunities without wasting time or money

It will all add up to a reliable method for generating promising business ideas that lead to profitable businesses, in just a weekend.

Let's dive in! This is where your taking action will pay off.

CHAPTER 3

Finding Million-Dollar Ideas

Simple Exercises to Generate Profitable Business Ideas

I didn't watch sports, and I don't like gambling, but I could spot a trend. Fantasy sports was getting huge, and so was sports betting. So my partners at the time and I decided to put together a fantasy sports betting site: BetArcade. We had all these sports game players on our Facebook app, and we thought we could push them toward a sports betting site. Easy money.

After six months of paying programmers to build the site—about $100,000—not to mention another $10,000 for lawyers to tell us that gambling online was legal, we launched. It was absolutely beautiful. Amazing graphics. Worked great.

And NO ONE CAME. Crickets.

Now we were truly screwed and money was running out. Then at our lowest point, we were broke and my desperation kicked in:

What was our biggest problem and did others share it? Was there a solution we were capable of creating quickly?

We were constantly complaining about how much we were

being charged by OfferPal, the payments provider for our successful games. They were charging 50 percent for every transaction and ignored EVERY upgrade suggestion we made. We *disliked* them strongly.

"You know, we could offer people a better margin if we just did it ourselves," I discussed with my business partner Andrew.

So I asked. Immediately, I called a few friends who owned Facebook games to see if they would switch to a different payment software if it offered lower commissions. Turns out it was an easy sell.

In a weekend, we put together a beta version of the site, and within two weeks after that we had the service called Gambit running. We instantly made our friends 20 percent more money by charging lower commissions and listening to them. In the first year, we ended up making more than $15 million in top-line revenue. It was insane.

The immediate success of this payments business that came from a moment of desperation—and in the wake of the failure of BetArcade—forced us to reckon with one of the most useful lessons of business creation: **It is deadly to build a business without first verifying that there are paying customers.**

Customers Want Solutions, Not Ideas

Customers don't care about your ideas; they care about whether you can solve their problems. And you should not build your idea into a business if you don't know with 100 percent certainty that it's a solution your customers will pay for.

Trust me, I've done that. After Disney verbally agreed to use an expanded version of our payment software for their social gaming ("Of course, we'd want something like that"), I was so certain of my brilliant idea that I went ahead and built

It is deadly to build a business without first verifying that there are paying customers.

it. Except six months later and $100,000 spent, they looked at what we delivered, said that however great it was, they didn't need it right away, and started ghosting me.

That's why, when it comes to generating business ideas, customers come first. *Before the product or service.* Even before the idea. **To build a business, you need someone to sell to.**

I can't tell you how many times someone has emailed me saying, "What do you think of this business idea?"

My auto-reply? "Have you asked what the customer thinks?"

Steve Jobs said, "You have to start with the customer experience and work backwards."

Jeff Bezos, too, insists everyone at Amazon use a Customer First Approach to generate ideas and decide which to develop. The first of *his* sixteen Leadership Principles—Customer Obsession—starts by saying, "Leaders start with the customer and work backwards."

Working backwards prioritizes access to a group of customers (a group you probably belong to) and focuses on an aspect of a customer's life that doesn't work.

If you do it this way, you're assured of nailing the three Ws of business right from the start:

- **Who** you are selling to
- **What** problem you're solving
- **Where** they are

Your goals in this chapter are to use the **Customer First** Approach, to narrow in on three markets that you'll target, to use your knowledge and experience of these markets to generate lots of ideas, and then to choose the three you think are the most likely to succeed.

It's the first step in the three-part Million Dollar Weekend process, in which you'll learn to sell ideas to a small early adopter group before you've built the product (or spent a cent) in order to validate that there is a market that will pay. Repeat, fast and cheap, until it hits.

Experiment, experiment, experiment—BOOM!

Start With What You Know. Or, How I Made $100 Million by Building "Groupon for Geeks"

When I started AppSumo a decade ago, I was a solopreneur living in a basement apartment in the Haight-Ashbury neighborhood of San Francisco. By day, I was consulting for an online dating site called SpeedDate. At night, I would rack my brain for business ideas.

Problem was, I'd had a series of businesses, like payments for social games, that had long sales processes that were hard to negotiate, and my company was a commodity. I wanted to move up the value chain to a place where people can't live without my product. The problem I was most interested in solving was how do I get more customers. Everyone in business is interested in more customers. I didn't want to do another business where my product was a *nice-to-have* (a vitamin)— I wanted to be a *must-have* (a painkiller). And getting more customers is the most essential business *need*.

One night I was thinking about a company called MacHeist that was offering bundles of Mac software at a steep discount. This was a great way for Mac users to get several useful apps at one really low price.

And while I love a good deal, I couldn't stop thinking about how MacHeist had solved the problem of providing companies with customers.

Every time MacHeist bundled software and marketed the bundle, it was solving a *need* of those software companies—customers—and in turn those software companies were doing everything they could in terms of marketing and blogging to make sure the MacHeist bundle was a success.

Could I do what MacHeist was doing but for non-Mac software?

> **PRO TIP:** Look for something working in one category and bring it to another. One of the largest drivers of AppSumo's email list was giveaways. We realized this only after seeing a giveaway in a women's fashion online site and trying it out ourselves. Sign up for and observe companies outside of your target market for inspiration.

As an entrepreneur, I'd come to rely on some of the flashy new web-based apps out there like Mailchimp (newsletters), Dropbox (storing files), and FreshBooks (accounting). With web-based software, it didn't matter what kind of computer you used as long as you had an internet connection.

But no one was offering discounted non-Mac bundles. Not yet! I was super-excited to get my favorite tools at a discount. There were other startup founders like me—tons! Now I had to find out the truth of whether people would pay me.

> **PRO TIP:** When in doubt, solve your own problems. If you are willing to pay for a solution, it's likely others are, too. And at least you'll have one happy customer—yourself.

I have always been active on Reddit. And I understood the community really well. I knew what its users liked and how they interacted with the site. Working backwards, I zeroed in on something all Redditors love: sharing images. At the time, more and more were relying on a new site called Imgur to host their viral meme images.

On Reddit's front page, every other post featured an image hosted on Imgur. While anyone could use Imgur for free, the company offered a pro subscription tier. Would these Redditors pay if I offered the pro tier at a deep discount?

At this point, I went to my mentor from my Facebook days, Doug Hirsch, who later founded GoodRX, to ask what he thought about the idea. He said it wouldn't work, that he didn't think there was enough software to make this a viable long-term business.

Don't let doubt from another dissuade you from finding out the truth. The only opinion that matters is your customer's. Your job, as a Customer First entrepreneur, is to listen to the problem your customers want solved, create a solution to it, and validate that they'll pay for it. No one else's.

With that realization, I jumped into Million Dollar Weekend validation mode.

Using the Ask muscle, I cold-emailed Imgur's creator, Alan Schaaf, who turned out to be a college student in Ohio, and asked him if he'd let me market pro subscriptions at a discount—and pay me for what I sold.

Here's exactly what I sent him:

SUBJECT: Promoting Imgur on Reddit
TO: Alan Schaff
FROM: Noah Kagan

Hey Alan

> Huge fan of Imgur and love using your product all the time.
>
> We are launching a deal site and wanted to promote your Imgur Pro.
>
> Think we can sell 200+ of it for you at no cost or work for you.
>
> You free Friday to chat on AIM at 5pm PT?
>
> Noah Kagan

He jumped at the idea because, well, I promised him money at no cost!

I had the three Ws of the business figured out:

- **Who:** Found an audience of potential customers? People on Reddit.
- **What:** Worked backwards to find a problem they wanted solved? Imgur Pro at a discount.
- **Where:** Time for me to flex the Ask muscle and pitch some Redditors? Game on!

Then I cold-emailed Chris Slowe, Reddit's founding engineer, and asked him to breakfast. After explaining what I planned to do over bacon—people love bacon—I asked Chris for free advertising. Not advice. Not a discount. Free ads.

Here's exactly what I said:

> SUBJECT: Hey Chris—friends with Chris Smoak
> TO: Chris Slowe
> FROM: Noah Kagan
>
> Hey Chris
>
> Talked with Chris Smoak and he says hi. I LOVE what you've built with Reddit. Huge user!

Wanted to treat you to a breakfast at Pork Store Cafe to give you some suggestions on the site and run by a cool promotion I'm working on with Imgur.

You free this Wed at 9am?

Be epic,
Noah Kagan

The original AppSumo.com homepage, built in 4 hours

"Why not?" Chris replied. "Our users love Imgur. They'll be thrilled to get a discount."

Now, creating a fully functional site for the deal would have cost money and time, so here's where it gets interesting:

I found a $12 an hour developer from Pakistan to help me add a PayPal button to a web page. That was 4 hours of work, and I did everything else on my own.

Total time to build AppSumo.com: 48 hours.

Total cost to build AppSumo.com: $50.

At the time, I had no idea if the business would work. My goal was to zero in on the one thing that matters: Would people pay for discounted software? If they didn't, the minimal investment I made would allow me to easily move on to the next experiment.

My ads went up on Reddit promoting the website I'd just built, and holy crap, my first sale arrived within minutes.

The first dollar is always the sweetest. It's momentum. It's possibility. It's fear getting its ass kicked.

> **PRO TIP: Focus on Zero to $1.** Get that first dollar. That will create your momentum and build your belief in what you're working on. Every company I started began with just one customer. Scaling comes later.

Before I knew it, I'd sold the 200 licenses I set as my goal. Who could have known this would lead to a company doing over $65 million just ten years later?

No Biz Plan Required

You might be familiar with the concept of the minimum viable product, or MVP. Instead of trying to develop something perfect and then unveiling it like Steve Jobs at Macworld, you create the simplest possible version of what you're offering and start selling it right away. That way, instead of endlessly refining something in a vacuum, you use feedback from actual customers to incrementally develop an offering people absolutely want to buy in the real world.

MVP is an important idea, but it leaves out something crucial: the customers. Who are you actually going to *sell* your minimum viable product to? And what if they don't *want* the minimum? What if they're willing to try something only from a full-fledged company with a name brand? Good luck iterating on your MVP without customers.

The problem with MVPs and older entrepreneurial approaches is, we get so fixated on what we want to make that we lose sight of the people who want it.

I call this the Founder First mentality, in which entrepreneurs focus on their own experience (*Yay, I get to build something!*) instead of Customer First.

Old school: You focus on business model planning and obsessing about the product at this stage.

New school: You're going to focus on the conversation with the customers, a dynamic back-and-forth that will help you iterate your product in terms of what the customer wants *before you make or spend a thing.*

One more example to make sure this is totally clear.

Okay, you have an idea for a dog-walking app. How would you go about doing it? Here's the way most people—most *wantrepreneurs*—would do it:

1. Spend hours at home thinking about the app (and coming up with clever names for it).
2. Spend $100 hiring their cousin to draw a cool logo.
3. Set up an LLC.
4. Watch YouTube videos about apps and programming and business. And dogs.
5. Consider signing up for a developer boot camp and quickly realize coding is hard.
6. Buy the domain name for the snazzy website they're going to build.

7. Look into hiring a developer on Upwork, and quickly realize it's prohibitively expensive.
8. Give up. Again.

Does that sound familiar? That's *Founder First*.

Okay. Now we are going to use a *Customer First Approach* to explore our idea for a dog-walking app:

1. Call or text three people right now who have dogs and ask them to pay you to walk their dog.
2. Turns out none of these dog owners have problems walking their dog. You discover their real problem is finding dog sitters when they're traveling.
3. Ask for their next travel dates and have them pay you a deposit. They pay: jackpot!

Pretty quickly you found out the opportunity was dog-sitting, not dog-walking. And now you have real customers paying you to solve a real problem, with real revenue flowing in, before writing a line of code or spending any money on freelancers.

That same framework applies across all industries and sectors.

At Sumo.com, we were having problems growing our email list. We contacted potential customers like Tim Ferriss and Pat Flynn, and it turns out they also found it challenging. Once we convinced a few customers to sign on, we built a suite of email collection tools for us, and them.

Or take Jennifer Jones, a Dallas elementary school teacher who was part of my Monthly1K class. Everyone liked her cookies. So she posted on Facebook saying she's making cookie baskets for the holidays. Did anyone want some? Turns out they *really* did, and she now has a $1,000 per month cookie business.

Jennifer posting to her Facebook page seeing if anyone is interested

Anybody who has a skill in something like that—homemade cakes, pickles, candles, you name it—can send an email to friends, family, coworkers, and church community members asking if they'd be interested in buying whatever it is. Include a PayPal link. Then fill all the orders you receive.

Voilà, a zero-risk business venture. No hiring, no website, no cooking school, no commercial kitchen. That stuff can come later, if at all. Just use the money you bring in to buy enough ingredients to fill the orders, bake the cakes, put them in boxes, and deliver them.

In each of these examples, the launch is not based on perfecting a business plan, but on talking to potential customers and finding out what they're excited to give you money for.

But where do you find those customers?

Now Where Do You Find Customers?

When novice entrepreneurs search for opportunities, they too often look beyond their **Zone of Influence**. They think the action is happening somewhere else, in some other location or industry. But seasoned entrepreneurs almost always find and create opportunities within the context of who they are, what they know, and especially who they know.

In each of the examples above, the business validation process begins with potential customers *in the entrepreneur's orbit*. Actual people with names. Tribes you belong to or are interested in, most of whom are already self-organized online. People you know how to reach, today.

Though it's rarely a part of their official origin stories, the biggest companies in the world—even the viral apps now worth billions—started through personal networks and real human connections.

Mark Zuckerberg started Facebook in a weekend by emailing friends to use it. Version 1 did well, validating it. And Microsoft started with Bill Gates building software for a guy in Albuquerque. He had a CUSTOMER FIRST.

In the beginning, founders should reach out to their friends, their former colleagues, their communities.

You may think your business is unique, but trust me, it's not. *Every successful business can start this way.*

For example, Anahita loves her dogs and wanted healthier snacks for them. She started taking her homemade organic dog treats to her local dog park. She would sell out every time. A year later she now has a store called the Barkery, a dog bakery.

Before you even think about picking a business idea, make sure you have easy access to the people you want to help. An easy way to do this is to think about where you have easy access to a targeted group of people whom you really want to help—like, say, new moms in Austin, cyclists, freelance writers, and taco obsessives (like me!).

> ### CHALLENGE
> #### Top three groups.
>
> Let's write out your top three groups to target.
>
> **Who do you have easy access to that you'd be EXCITED to help?** This can be your neighbors, colleagues, religious friends, golf buddies, cooking friends, etc.
>
> _____
>
> _____
>
> _____

The better you understand your target group, the better you can speak to them. The more specifically you can speak to their problems, the better and easier you can sell (or test products).

Note how this process prioritizes communication with people, through starting (taking the first iteration of your solution straight to customers) and asking (engaging them in a conversation to determine how your solution can best fix their problem). **Business creation should always be a conversation!**

Nearly every impulse we have is to be tight with our ideas by doing more research, going off alone to build the perfect product—anything and everything to avoid the discomfort of asking for money. This is the validation shortcut. You have to learn to fight through this impulse. It won't be easy, but it'll be worth it.

Become a Problem Seeker

The best entrepreneurs are the most dissatisfied. They're always thinking of how things can be better.

Your frustrations—and the frustrations of others—are your business opportunities.

Great ideas come from being a problem seeker. Analyze frustrations in your day, including the things that bother you at home, waste your time on your commute to work, or online.

Here's a list of things that bother me:

- What to make for breakfast that's quick, healthy, and full of caffeine
- How to find a reliable house cleaner
- Where to go to dinner with my partner
- How to find my next therapist
- What kind of investment to make with some extra cash I received

And these are just the problems I've encountered today. I could go on and on... and that's the point!

The number of things that can be better are endless—which is a gold mine for newbie entrepreneurs. **The crucial first step toward entrepreneurship is to study your own unhappiness and to think of solutions (aka business opportunities) for you to sell.**

Look at this email my friend Boris Korsunsky sent when he was validating a private chef service (he doesn't even know how to cook!).

> SUBJECT: Helping you, help me with food!
>
> Hey Friends
>
> One thing I realized is that I'm busy all the time and I don't have time to cook a quality meal. :(
>
> I wanted to invite a few close friends to test a business idea with me.
>
> Consider yourself the lucky chosen few. :)
>
> Convenient and home-cooked meals.
>
> On February 9, for $20, there will be a personal chef making us food and delivering it to you conveniently and deliciously!
>
> If this is something you're seriously interested in, please paypal $20.
>
> Open to all and any feedback.
>
> Cheers,
> Boris
> P.S. Please let me know if you have any dietary restrictions, or any particular preferences. I promise the dinner will be delish!!!

Boris got five plus sales from this email, and an opportunity was born! Notice how Boris framed this as helping solve the problem of people like himself who didn't have time to cook? Smart boy, that Boris.

I built AppSumo because I couldn't find great discounts on the best business apps; our team built SumoMe because we needed a tool to grow our email list; we launched TidyCal.com because we were tired of monthly subscriptions of competitors; and there's more.

Other businesses I built all started with a frustration: not being able to find a good community to talk about social networks in the Bay Area (CommunityNext), or a good in-game payment service (Gambit), or weights for my home gym during the COVID pandemic.

Solving my own problems built a business that generates literally $65 million per year. I'm not saying that to brag (even though it does feel good to say), but to keep reminding you how simple yet effective this process can be. You can do this.

The Idea Generators

So let's open the net wide and get down to generating ideas... I mean problems!

Here's what the process of coming up with a million-dollar business idea does NOT look like:

- Getting on TikTok or YouTube and mindlessly copying whatever the influencers say is working for them
- Getting struck with the perfect vision for a genius new product
- Meditating, following your passion, and brainstorming
- Following any other woo-woo method that promises inspiration in a box

Here's what the actual process looks like:

1. What's the most painful (aka valuable) problem you can solve for people...

2. That you also have passion for and/or unique expertise in...

3. For the largest niche possible that you belong to and understand...

Simple enough, but takes some light and fun brainwork.

Remember to focus on your Zone of Influence here (your existing community): the 150 followers you have on TikTok, the 200 in your local Taco Aficionados group, the 300 in the WhatsApp group for your mountain biking club (not to mention the 143,000 in the subreddit r/mountainbiking). Your job as a problem seeker is to go to a community of yours.

You can access all the idea challenges and more examples at MillionDollarWeekend.com.

Now it's your turn. Use the following **four challenges** to come up with at least ten potentially profitable ideas:

1. Solve Your Own Problems

Take entrepreneur Shane Heath, a dude who loved coffee, but hated that it made him anxious and jittery. Everyone around him kept saying, "I want to cut down on coffee, too." But no one was quitting coffee—because there was nothing better to drink!

Then Shane went to India and discovered masala chai. Shane loved it: It tasted great and gave him a small caffeine kick. But it didn't make him feel like a vibrating wreck like coffee did.

So Shane invented Mud/Wtr. His Mud is a masala chai coffee replacement with other ingredients for added health benefits.

When he walked around with his mug of Mud, people wanted to know what he was drinking. So he made some for his friends—and it got them hooked.

That tiny problem of his is now making over $60 million per year!

When you intentionally practice problem-spotting, eventually it becomes something your mind just does automatically. It's become a game to me—a profitable one.

Still stuck? Here are four questions to get you going:

1. What is one thing this morning that irritated me?
2. What is one thing on my to-do list that's been there over a week?
3. What is one thing that I regularly fail to do well?
4. What is one thing I wanted to buy recently only to find out that no one made it?

I make it a habit to always keep a notebook close by and jot down things that bother me. Below are three of my most recent business opportunities:

FIND ME AN X

How I thought of it: I spent a ton of time trying to buy a car. About a year. I know! Online research, visiting car dealerships, test drives, on and on. Anyway, I would have paid a pretty penny for someone to hear all my thoughts and preferences, do the research and conversations for me, and produce a short document with the three best choices.

Idea: You can pick a vertical where people can give you requirements and you find whatever they are looking for.

CHEAP AND REMOTE INTERIOR DESIGN FOR YOUNG SINGLE GUYS

How I thought of it: Until I was thirty, I never had my own place, so my furniture has always been a weird collection of IKEA items. Really easy having a cool place when you're loaded; not so easy, but possible, when your budget is tight.

Idea: Interior designers are for rich people. This business would be much simpler (and less expensive): I send someone a photo of my place, giving my preferences, and they put together a Pinterest page of suggestions for me.

FRIEND/ACTIVITY MATCHMAKER

How I thought of it: I love doing paddleboarding and going to the gym, but my friends aren't always available.

Idea: Meetup is good for groups, but it'd be nice if some person or website could connect me with individuals to join me on these activities. Lately I've been wanting new activity partners for things I'm doing. The website or service would be similar to Meetup but more on the individual level.

CHALLENGE

Solve your own problems.

Use the questions to find three ideas. Write those down in your MDW Journal or here in the book.

_____

_____

_____

---

2. Bestsellers Are Your Best Friends

What products are *already* selling a crap-ton? iPads, iPhones, etc. Basically, any product you'd find on Amazon's Bestseller list would work here.

How can you accessorize the product (for example, stickers for an iPhone) or sell a service to those people (teaching someone how to use an iPhone)?

It's easier to sell to a large group of people who've already spent money on a product or service.

Some ideas could be:

1. Customizing Nike shoes.
2. Video game tutorial for an Xbox game.
3. Teaching computer novices how to use a MacBook.

> **CHALLENGE**
>
> **Bestsellers are your best friends.**
>
> Write down two accessorizing ideas in your MDW Journal or here in the book.
>
> _____
>
> _____

PS: Don't worry if this method doesn't inspire you to idea glory. Remember: This is just an exercise. That means anything goes—you have my blessing to write down all the bad, crazy, and nonsense ideas that come into your mind. DO NOT EDIT YOURSELF. Do not think, *But how could that work?* Just write as many down as you can. We'll whittle them down later.

3. Marketplaces

One of my favorite ways to find ideas is by studying the marketplaces where people are TRYING to spend money. Your potential customers are everywhere already asking in public for solutions—on message boards, in Facebook posts, in tweets, in church groups, on and on!

Marketplaces on Craigslist, Etsy, or Facebook have millions of people each day wanting to pay to have their problems solved. So look for frequent requests on Craigslist gigs from people actively searching for someone to give their money to in exchange for particular services.

Check completed listings on eBay. This allows you to see how well certain products are selling. It's also an easy way to measure the sale prices of items and gauge the overall percentage of the market that's receiving bids.

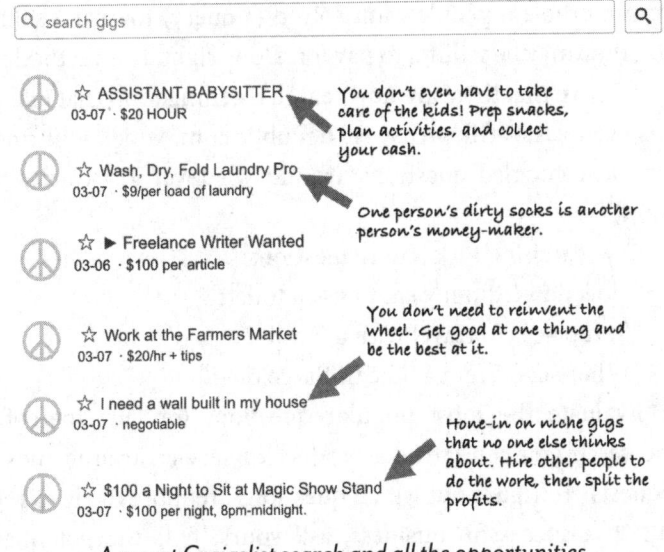

A recent Craigslist search and all the opportunities

> ### CHALLENGE
> #### Marketplaces.
> Visit a marketplace like Etsy, Facebook Marketplace, Craigslist, or eBay and write at least one idea for a product or service in your MDW Journal or here in the book.

Finding Million-Dollar Ideas | 61

4. Search Engine Queries

It's much easier to sell something when people ALREADY want it. There are 3 billion Google searches every day, giving you a direct line to customers' thoughts and needs.

To access these thoughts, you'll want to work backwards from a problem people want solved (a query) toward a solution they may be willing to pay for. Done right, this method is so effective that there are now search listening tools that make this even easier (like AnswerThePublic.com, which will find the most googled questions around whatever keyword you input).

Try searching for certain questions:

"How do I train my cat to use a toilet?"

"Best places to travel with a family?"

"Where can I rent a bike in Barcelona?"

Evaluate the most popular questions (or lack thereof) and see if you can create a product or service around those requests. To figure out which questions are more likely to result in a successful business, ask yourself: Is the potential solution a vitamin (a nice-to-have) or a painkiller (a must-have)?

I also use Reddit.com as a gold mine for business ideas. It is one of the largest message boards online. Go to the r/SomebodyMakeThis subreddit where people are ACTIVELY offering up ideas and look for the first two things that interest you.

| 🔍 how do i train my cat to | ✕ | 📷 |

🔍 how do i train my cat to **use the toilet**
🔍 how do i train my cat to **walk on a leash**
🔍 how do i train my cat to **stay off the counter**
🔍 how do i train my cat to **stop biting**
🔍 how do i train my cat to **be a therapy cat**
🔍 how do i train my cat to **sit**
🔍 how do i train my cat to **not bite**
🔍 how do i train my cat to **sleep with me**
🔍 how do i train my cat to **be an outdoor cat**
🔍 how do i train my cat to **stay indoors**

An example from a Google search for all the cat lovers out there

---

CHALLENGE

Search engine queries.

Use search engine questions and Reddit forums to find two more ideas. Write them in your MDW Journal or here in the book.

_____

_____

You should now have a list of ten ideas, if not many more. You can also use the business idea you asked a friend for in chapter 1.

Use the four challenges (solve your own problems, bestsellers, marketplaces, and search engine queries).

Here's a place to write your ten ideas:

Finding Million-Dollar Ideas

1. _____
2. _____
3. _____
4. _____
5. _____
6. _____
7. _____
8. _____
9. _____
10. _____

Now you've got to pick the three best ideas from the ten plus you've come up with.

There's never a "perfect" idea. For instance, AppSumo started out selling bundles of web tools and three years later evolved to individual deals, our own custom software, and our own courses. Your idea will evolve over time, just as all businesses do.

So here's what you're going to do: take your list of ten plus ideas, and eliminate the ones that you're not excited about.

If the top three ideas are screaming, "Me! Me! Me!" your work is done.

If you can't decide, choose the ones you believe will be easiest to implement—and that you (and ideally other customers) would be thrilled to spend money on.

That's it!

Don't worry if you think your ideas suck or are too hard. The real value is learning to create, assess, and validate ideas. In the next chapter, you'll learn how to determine whether you have a million-dollar opportunity on your hands.

CHAPTER 4

The One-Minute Business Model

Shape Your Idea into a Million-Dollar Opportunity

"Fine!" I said. "Watch *me* do it!"

My Monthly1K students were worrying because none of them had actually made their first $1,000 yet. They would get excited to start, but chicken out when it came time to actually sell their product.

I wanted to show you that it didn't have to be scary. "I'll come up with an idea and make $1,000 in profit this week," I told them. I saw them laughing and scoffing.

Marco, the one who I'd pegged as the leader, turned to me. "We really respect you, Noah," he said. "But a week's a long time. That sounds too easy for a guy like you. How about twenty-four hours, and we get to choose your idea?"

The others nodded.

I had to laugh. The cojones on these people!

"Fine, man. Game ON."

So we came to an agreement: I could pick any of the businesses suggested by my students, but I couldn't use my

AppSumo networks and mailing lists to promote it. I had to do this like anybody who didn't have a big social media following.

Five minutes later, a flood of ideas came in. The three most interesting business ideas my students suggested were lemonade, salsa, and beef jerky.

Now, I like lemonade.

I really like salsa.

But I LOVE jerky.

More important, I KNOW jerky. I already was spending about $50 a month on the stuff and figured at least some of my health-conscious friends were spending that amount, too.

I assumed they were struggling like me to find different flavors and different brands, even with the dozens of new jerky artisans popping up every month to try to satisfy our needs. It was likely a growing multimillion-dollar market.

Still, I was nervous. Would I be able to make $1,000 in twenty-four hours, without using my existing resources? The pressure was on.

I'll walk you through the jerky experiment over the next two chapters to show how everything I'm about to teach you helped me create a business in one day that we sold for $120,000 two years later. (If we had kept going, it could have hit seven figures, but I wanted to move on and keep experimenting.) In this chapter, you'll go through a three-part process to verify that your startup has the potential to be a million-dollar business, including my process for pivoting your business model (as I had to in hour 12 of the jerky experiment) if something's not working quite right.

Here is what you'll learn:

1. **"Is this a million-dollar opportunity?"** You'll research the market to find out.

2. **"What's my model?"** You'll create a simple budget by sketching out revenue, cost, and profit, so you know how many units you'll need to sell and for how much to make $1 million.
3. **"What if it turns out it's not going to work?"** You'll pivot and evolve: You'll use customer feedback to adjust the variables of the business (pricing, model, offer, category—all that) into something bigger and better.

You have limited resources to pursue the ideas you believe are winners. And if you're going to work hard either way, might as well work on the idea with the most upside.

So think of this chapter as a tactical approach to finding winners. You're going to narrow down your three ideas from the last chapter into one—one that's got a solid business model and a market full of growth potential.

Step 1. Find $1 Million Worth of Customers

You, dear reader, are a surfer. What you're selling—the product or service—is your surfboard. The market is the wave, and the wave is what matters most.

Even if you're a great surfer with an amazing board, you will still fail if you don't have a good wave to ride.

A tidal wave would be ideal, but any good big wave is just fine.

Now, don't think that finding a great wave means you have to be in Hot New Tech. You can find awesome waves everywhere. If you are in the midst of a big underserved lawn-care market, then landscaping is a Big Wave Business—seriously!

Take New York City's professional line sitter, Robert Samuel.

After getting fired from his customer service job at AT&T, he noticed the frenzy created by every new iPhone release. So he put an ad on Craigslist in 2012 to validate whether anyone would pay for him to wait in line. When he was paid $325 for his first fifteen-hour stint, he knew he had a wave.

Today, his business Same Ole Line Dudes (SOLD) employs thirty dudes and dudettes, charging a $50 minimum up to two hours and $25 for each additional hour to wait in line for everything from hot new sneakers to the DMV to the newest iPhone release—and Robert himself takes home *$80,000 a year*.

An advertisement from Robert

There are countless waves you can ride that have nothing to do with tech. Codie Sanchez has gained over 1 million followers on social media because she teaches people how to own and operate "boring businesses" like vending machines and RV rentals.

A good wave isn't about being cool; it's about having customers. **What I'm saying here is that your job is not to create demand for something that seems exciting, it's to find existing demand and satisfy it.**

You can have the absolute best idea in the world—or something that seems like it—and end up not selling one single thing if there's no demand.

You don't want to be convincing people that they need your product. You don't want to be begging them to buy. What you want when you're opening a taco restaurant is a starving crowd.

When I look back over my life, being involved in Tidal Wave Markets—big and growing and with massive momentum—has been a huge part of my success, and it's something I now prioritize when I think about new businesses.

Facebook? Huge adoption of college students and the world wanting to connect online.

Mint? Huge market of people wanting a free finance tool to save and make more money.

Kickflip? Facebook and iPhone opened up their platforms for apps and games, leading to a huge surge for game developers.

Gambit? With all the games that were launched, everyone needed payment options.

And I launched AppSumo just as the world decided to be entrepreneurs—and needed software to make it possible.

When I started AppSumo.com, there were only about

In order to have a million-dollar business, you need a million-dollar opportunity.

twenty software tools we could promote. But over the next ten years the market of people buying and making software exploded. That gave me a much easier opportunity to create a $65 million revenue business.

Now, it won't always be that easy. Not a lot of private businesses publish their sales data. But there are plenty of other ways to make sure you're surfing a good wave.

The rule here?

In order to have a million-dollar business, you need a million-dollar opportunity.

It's that simple. Thing is, how do you prove you have one?

Too often aspiring entrepreneurs think they need spreadsheets and extensive research to figure this out. These are just a distraction. Let me show you a better way.

Here's a market opportunity exercise. Say you have a beard or love someone who does. The problem: Beards are itchy! Before you spend months of tinkering to create the world's greatest beard oil, let's figure out if you can really make a million dollars from this idea—see if there's a business here.

There are two key questions to answer to make sure it's a million-dollar opportunity:

1. Is the overall market dying, flat, or growing? You want flat or ideally growing!
2. Is this a million-dollar opportunity? To figure that out, we have to know the number of potential customers and the price of your product.

First, I would check to see if there are enough customers who'd want to buy your beard oil. Market size is the single most important variable to quickly understanding the potential of any project.

I use Google Trends and Facebook Ads to answer those questions. They're great tools that help me evaluate the size and growth potential of my target market.

It's possible that the tools will change, but the idea is to uncover the data that shows how big and growing your market is by answering the following questions:

1. **Is the market growing or dying?** Search Google Trends for the terms "beard" and "beard grooming" and compare their search popularity to similar terms (for example, "haircuts," "razors") and how that's changed over the last few months and years. With Google Trends you are just looking to see how the graphs are trending – ideally up and to the right.

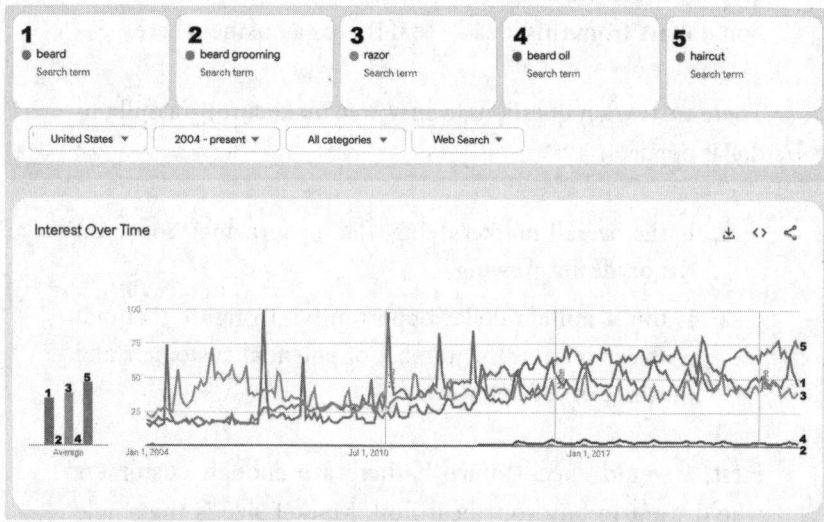

A Google Trends search to show interest in different beard terms

2. **How many potential customers are there?** I'd highly recommend using Facebook Ads to research your market size. Facebook is pretty much the entire world, and what's phenomenal is that they actually let you type in the keyword of whatever business category you're thinking about and see the approximate audience size. You can also use the Facebook Ads Library to see every single active ad running on Facebook for your keyword and location, which is super helpful for uncovering competitors and getting ideas for your own marketing efforts.

To see videos of me doing this analysis, go to MillionDollarWeekend.com.

Searching "beards" shows us the number of people interested in beards on Facebook in the United States = 16 to 19 million. Not bad, not bad.

And for "beard oil"?

Something like 2.5 million people. Score!

Now, you can also use these tools to focus on even more specific angles. For instance, take some other groups you could think of targeting:

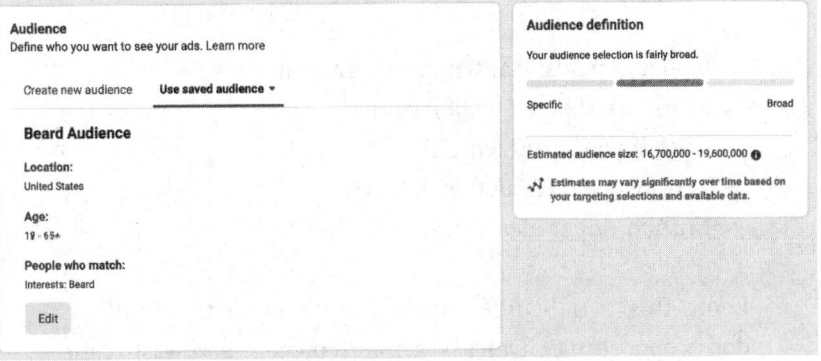

A search for "beards" on Facebook Ads targeting

- Locals: Beard owners in local cities
- More niche: Narrow interest groups like ingrown facial hair
- Demographics-based: African American beard owners

Step 2. Is This a Million-Dollar Opportunity?

When I was starting my Ninja discount card at UC Berkeley, there were only 25,000+ students on campus, and I was confident I could sell my discount card for $10. At best this could be a $250,000 business only if I was PERFECT. If I expanded to all the major college campuses in California, I could reach a student market of 1 million. It was clear this could easily create a million-dollar business.

Here are the major things you're looking for:

- Pick a price point you think will be ideal for your customer.
- Multiply that by the number of ideal customers.
- Does that equal at least a million dollars? Yes or no?

Simple!

Now let's evaluate that on our beard oil idea:

- Google Trends: Flat with some growth
- Size of market: 2,500,000 people
- Cost of your product: $50
- Total Value: $125,000,000
- Million-dollar idea? YES!

Look, this is a SUPER-simple way to evaluate a million-dollar opportunity. Don't be a wantrepreneur and waste time calculating revenue to the exact cent or fretting about the optimal price point. We are just trying to see if this is a million-dollar idea, super-fast. Let's do some other examples.

Setting up people's home offices idea
- Google Trends: Significantly up
- Size of market: 50,000 people
- Cost of your product: $500
- Total Value: $25,000,000
- Million-dollar idea? YES!

In the words of the great DJ Khaled, "Another one!" But that's not always the case.

Monthly Vietnamese pho broth subscription idea
- Google Trends: Little interest and no growth
- Size of market: 1,000 people
- Cost of your product: $20
- Total Value: $20,000
- Million-dollar idea? No.

I'm sorry if you love making pho broth and want to deliver it, but I wouldn't touch this business idea because I don't see enough demand for it! It could be a fun passion project, but it's not a million-dollar business.

Here are four examples to compare:

Data/ Business Idea	Home Office Setup	Nonalcoholic Drink Subscriptions	Juicy Ass Pho Broth	Crypto Taxes
Google Trends	Significantly up	Significantly up	Up	Rocket ship
Size of market	50,000	50,000	1,000	50,000

Cost	$500	$200	$20	$250
Market opportunity	$25,000,000	$10,000,000	$20,000	$12,500,000
Worth pursuing?	YES	YES	NO	YES

See 10+ more step-by-step examples for business ideas at MillionDollarWeekend.com.

All you want is to know if the business idea is worth pursuing. Now that we know it's worth it, let's confirm how exactly you're going to get your million dollars.

To do that, we'll use the One-Minute Business Model.

Step 3. The One-Minute Business Model

Many people have asked me to review their business plan. I always give the same advice: "Your plan is to make money!"

Realistically you're not going to get 5 or 10 percent of this market, BUT now let's see what it would take to generate your own $1 million in profit.

Revenue − Cost = Profit. These determine if you can make your first million dollars.

> **Revenue (all the money you make) − Cost (how much it costs to make it) = Profit (what you get to take home)**

This is obviously extremely basic, but that's the point. It's all you need to calculate in order to assess whether you can get to $1 million.

Let's plug in some numbers to see how it works, continuing with our beard oil example:

Our Beard oil sells for	$ 50.00
Cost to make, package, and ship	$ 37.50
Profit per unit sold	**$ 12.50**

You may be worrying about advertising costs, optimal pricing, manufacturers, what happens when all your customers' beards look so gorgeous ... I know. This is the fear in you worrying about too many things. What we are looking for are rough estimates. Momentum is your friend, and we can sweat the details later. For now, let's focus on the high-level stuff to see the potential in your business.

If you're able to earn $12.50 in profit for every unit sold, then it's easy to calculate how many you'll need to sell to make $1,000,000. You just divide your target profit by the profit:

Target Profit	$ 1,000,000
Profit per unit sold	$ 12.50
Total sales needed	**80,000**

Okay, obviously selling 80,000 units sounds hard AF, but consider the following:

- This is ONLY the number of people we see via Facebook.
- This is for only one beard product. If you find success with beard oil, you can easily repeat the process many times with other grooming products.
- This is only the first sale to these customers. It's far easier to sell to an existing customer than it is to acquire new ones, so once we've built up a decent customer base, we can make even more products to sell to them.

- Plus, you can likely sell a subscription to increase the amount you sell per customer.

By all measures, it appears that we have a million-dollar idea on our hands. Actually, I know for a fact that it is—my good friend who founded Beardbrand.com has a multimillion-dollar company doing the above.

It's not always so simple. Sometimes you'll be playing with the numbers and realize you'll need to rethink some aspects of the business, as I did early on in the jerky challenge.

After accepting the challenge from my business students and spending around three minutes deciding to call it Sumo Jerky after everybody vetoed noahsajerk.com, I was on the StairMaster at the gym talking to my colleague Anton, discussing how easy this would be when I started the next morning.

"Dude, this is going to be cake. Jerky is healthy, and it's really popular," I said.

But a few hours later in bed, around midnight, I got swamped by a wave of anxiety and thought, *I've got only twenty-four hours! If I fail, this is going to be really embarrassing.*

I jumped out of bed to rerun the numbers. The One-Minute Business Model saved my ass by showing me I needed to pivot my business.

I'd been planning to sell a month of jerky for $20 because that seemed like a reasonable price I'd personally be willing to pay.

From a few searches online, I found I could source jerky at about $10 per order and it would cost around $5 to ship each order.

1 Bag of Jerky	$ 20
Cost to acquire, package, and ship	$ 15
Profit	$ 5

Uh-oh ... That meant:

Target profit	$ 1,000
Profit per unit sold	$ 5
Total sales needed	200

Two hundred bags of jerky in twenty-four hours?!

Oof, too many sales in too little time!

After I realized that I'd never make my Sumo Jerky goal selling one-off deliveries, I went back to the drawing board. That got me thinking of other businesses I launched, like my conference series, CommunityNext.

Back when I was in the conference business, I started by selling individual tickets, which worked but required tons of effort. That stumped me until I thought, *Oh, I can make a lot more money just selling package sponsorships to companies, who can then hand out tickets to employees or customers.* That in turn got me thinking about the equivalent of sponsorships in the jerky world.

How do I do bigger deals per transaction?

What about a subscription service?

If I could sell subscriptions, I could dramatically cut the number of sales I needed to make. If they were all three-month subscriptions, I'd need to sell only 67. And six-month? Only 33.

I also realized that if I sold to offices that offered snacks, it would be easier to find customers with larger disposable budgets. Plus, I figured I had a lot of close friends at companies who could buy for their employees or refer me to their office managers.

> **PRO TIP:** When you're launching a business, always ask yourself: is this going to be a one-off purchase, something customers buy here and there when they want to consume it, or can you make it a monthly recurring sale?

> It's always better to be in the reorder business.
> —John Paul Jones DeJoria, founder of
> Paul Mitchell and Patrón Spirits

With the clock ticking on my 24-hour challenge, let's see what happened next!

Step 4. Pivot and Evolve— Your Revenue Dials

Almost every successful business had to pivot or change course along the way. Maybe you chose the wrong market to begin with. Or maybe one feature of your offer turns out to be the thing people want. Just keep your eyes open for adjacent opportunities.

The easiest way for me to reach my goal was to increase the average order value by selling longer-term subscriptions to businesses.

My One-Minute Business Model changed to this:

6-month subscription	$ 120
Product cost	$ 60
Shipping	$ 30
Profit	$ 30

Now I needed to make only 33 sales ($1,000 target profit/$30 profit) to make this happen. Way more doable than the target of 200!

By tweaking the Revenue Dials, I could potentially make Sumo Jerky work. Here are the six **Revenue Dials** you can use:

1. **Average order value:** Increase the amount someone purchases.
2. **Frequency:** Increase how often someone will buy your service.
3. **Price point:** Increase or decrease your price point to affect total sales.
4. **Customer type:** Approach a more lucrative/wealthier customer segment.
5. **Product line:** Add additional products to make the business more attractive to start.
6. **Add-on services:** If you're selling a product like cookies, can you offer a service like setting up birthday parties or cooking at the person's home?

Examples of Pivots
- AppSumo started as bundle software for Silicon Valley startups but moved to selling individual deals to marketing agencies.

- Gambit started out making sports games on Facebook but found the real opportunity in payments for social games instead.
- Sam Parr's thehustle.co went from throwing live events to focusing just on the newsletter they used to promote the events. Fun fact: that newsletter business sold to HubSpot for a high eight figures.

The Million-Dollar Opportunity Challenge

For the challenge of this chapter, we're going to see whether your idea is a million-dollar opportunity.

Now which business idea to pick? The first one on your list!

The hard part is not choosing which business idea. The hard part is getting customers. And that's where you'll focus first.

The real goal here is less which idea is golden and more putting in the reps of checking market size before we validate later. If your first idea passes the million-dollar opportunity test, perfect. Proceed to the next chapter.

If not, then move on to your next idea and run it through the same assessment. Don't get in your own way, wondering which idea is best.

1. Pick one business idea.
2. Make sure it's a million-dollar opportunity.
3. Confirm your business idea is profitable.

If you're still stuck on how to do this and don't just want to choose the first idea on the list, then start with the problem that is most exciting for you to solve yourself.

The idea you are going to do: _____

Let's check the market size:

Data/Business Idea	Home Office Setup	Your Idea
Google Trends	Significantly up	
Size of market (via Facebook Ads)	50,000	
Cost	$500	
Market opportunity	**$25,000,000**	
Worth Pursuing?	**yes**	

If your idea is worth pursuing, now we have to make sure it's profitable.

Calculate your profit:

	Home Office Setup	Your Idea
Price	$ 500	
Cost	$ 25	
Profit	**$ 475**	

Then let's see if YOU can make a million dollars doing this business:

	Home Office Setup	Your Idea
Your target profit	$1,000,000	
Profit per unit sold	$475	
Total sales needed	2,105	

See a video walk-through of the entire process at MillionDollarWeekend.com.

The One-Minute Business Model | 83

Two thousand one hundred and five home office sales seem like a lot. Maybe not if you have a huge following about home offices; if you're just getting started, you may want to pivot your idea or consider a new one. This process saves you the time from working on ideas with little potential. Feel free to use this on a few of your ideas to compare the opportunities. Your dream may not be making a million dollars. This exercise helps you recognize your likelihood of succeeding to whatever Freedom Number you want!

With twelve hours left before the clock ran out on Sumo Jerky, it was time to talk to customers and see if I could really generate $1,000 in profit. Let's go get some customers for your business.

CHAPTER 5

The 48-Hour Money Challenge

Validate Your Business by Getting Paid

Yes, jerky. No, you're not a jerk. I'm literally selling jerky. Three-, six-, and twelve-month packages to companies just like yours. Which one do you want? AMAZING—you're in for a twelve-month at SendGrid. I love you. Can you PayPal me right now at paypal@okdork.com? Cool—expect your office mates to worship you when I ship it out in the next few weeks!"

This was me all day long. Slinging jerky like I had a 24-hour challenge, 'cause I did!

Here's also an example of an email I sent to Zach, who was one of the first purchasers (note the time it was sent).

SUBJECT: question for today.   2:01 am
TO: Zack
FROM: Noah Kagan

im testing out a new venture. figured you'd like it:

monthly jerky service.

$40/month is enough for healthy jerky every single mother fricking day, about $1.42/day *for delicious snackage.*

trying to sell blocks of 3 ($120) or 6 ($240) months.

you in?

limiting to 20sh people today so i can place a bulk order for next week.

===> paypal@okdork.com

XOXO

noah

ps. know any offices who buy snacks i should chat it up with???

It was a long day. And after working my ass off, here are the final Sumo Jerky numbers:

- **$4,040 in total revenue**
- **$1,135 in profit!!!**

Not bad for a guy who got fired from Facebook and was in English as a second language.

(One thing you may be wondering is how I got the jerky. When you have money from customers, fulfillment is easy. Be worried when it's the other way around. I searched and contacted people via Google and Instagram to sell me their jerky at the prices I had listed.)

Now at this point, you have successfully verified that your own idea has million-dollar-potential.

Now it's time to test whether people will actually spend money on your product.

This step is c-r-i-t-i-c-a-l. A lot of your ideas will seem great in theory, but you'll never know if they can go from *idea* to *business* until you actually test your target market's willingness to pay.

For instance, when I was launching AppSumo, I wasn't 100 percent convinced people wanted to buy software deals online similar to Groupon. So I had to validate AppSumo's business model by seeing if I could get paying customers.

Validation is *finding three customers in forty-eight hours who will give you money for your idea.*

The AppSumo validation worked really well, and since I discovered the power of validating when founding AppSumo, I've used the Validation process for every business venture I've started—including Sumo Jerky.

What I discovered using the Validation process was that once you understand it, you can apply it to any and every business idea—no matter how small or trivial.

Every potential business idea can be instantly verified, like your own magic wand.

The benefits of Validation are immediate and critical:

1. You don't waste time.
2. You save money.
3. You find out if you can actually get customers for your idea.
4. You get money up front.
5. You light a fire under your butt to get moving.

And by saving time and money, Validation will ultimately allow you to test as many of your ideas as possible. Theoretically you can test fifty-two ideas per year—COMFORTABLY—but that's not necessary because this method will likely take you only three to five weekends at most before you strike gold!

The Golden Rule of Validation

Much like the Validation process my Monthly1K students made me use for Sumo Jerky, to validate, I turn to the Golden Rule of Validation:

Find three customers in forty-eight hours who will give you money for your idea.

Success means moving quickly and spending no money. And that's what makes the Golden Rule of Validation so effective. Here's why it works so well:

- **You're allowed only forty-eight hours.** Limitations breed creativity. Having a tight time limit will cut off the doubting wantrepreneur inside you and force you to iterate fast and be creative until you find something that works.
- **Get your first three customers.** Your first customer is a friend, the second customer is someone in your family, but your third customer is HARD. You think this is easy? Then get three customers. Don't worry about building a business, we are ONLY validating your idea. And if it's this hard now, it'll ONLY get harder.
- **Collect money up front.** The *promise* of payment is not validation. That's polite rejection. Getting customers to hand over their dollars makes it real. But you need to get real money, from real people. Services like PayPal, Stripe, Cash App, and Venmo make collecting it easy these days.

The point is, if you can get someone to give you money quickly just by describing a product or solution, you're good!

You're not trying to invent demand; you're trying to see how EXCITED people are about what you're helping them with.

Three Methods to Validate ANY Business Idea

1. Direct Preselling

My favorite way to validate the market for a product is to make real contact with real people, tell them what I'm selling, ask for money, and see how they react. Actively preselling your first few customers is the best way for entrepreneurs to launch a business.

My friend Eric booked $8,000 of business in two weeks by knocking on doors and handing people a flyer, saying, "Hey, how's it goin'? I'm Eric with Foothills Painting. I noticed you had some peeling paint up here on your house, so I wanted to give you a free estimate."

That two-sentence pitch built him a $750,000-a-year business.

Or take what happened to Dana, a typical wantrepreneur who enrolled in my Monthly1K course to start a horse-industry business. She turned away from building a costly app and used the preselling method to quickly and cheaply validate instead.

Here's the exact conversation that changed her perspective:

> DANA: I am doing a horses business. We are launching in four months. Going to do this thing with horses and trainers and then I have a guy who's a professional.
>
> NOAH: Okay.

DANA: Yeah, so we are looking for a developer and funding to build our prototype.

NOAH: Okay, so what is the actual problem you are solving?

DANA: Well, I've taken a ton of Skillshare classes, I'm doing customer research, and we are working with a developer to get the site launched in four months.

NOAH: Again, what is the actual problem you are solving?

DANA: We want to help teach people how to take care of horses.

NOAH: YES! Now we are getting somewhere!! So what do people do today and what's wrong with it?

DANA: The YouTube videos are crappy. Horse people have tons of money and don't have access to great knowledge.

NOAH: SNAPS. So how can you prove that people will actually pay to have this problem solved?

DANA: I can message people in my horse groups and friends to see if they'll give me money for that expert knowledge.

NOAH: Now we are talking.

Dana officially made her first dollar (actually $1,000) the first week she went live with her "test" by messaging friends and people in her horse group. She didn't need a full-blown website or application to start the business. Heck, she didn't even have a company bank account or an LLC corporation—just a PayPal (or Venmo or Cash App or real dollars!) for the first few months.

Your Dream Ten List for Preselling

You learned about the Customer First Approach in chapter 3. Now, using that knowledge, we are going to create the first ten people you're going to contact for preselling.

Your aim is to determine which ones are likely to be the easiest to be your ideal customers. With them, you'll get the fastest zero to $1.

To start, I create a spreadsheet with ten rows. These are going to be your Dream Ten prospects: ideal people you want to validate your business idea with.[1]

Here are the columns to use:

Name	Company	Phone	Email	When contacted	When to follow up	Notes

You can grab a free Dream Ten spreadsheet at MillionDollarWeekend.com.

---

[1] The Dream Ten is inspired by Chet Holmes, who came up with the idea of the Dream 100 buyers strategy and writes about it in *The Ultimate Sales Machine*.

Make it easy: start with your best friends who might be interested—your Zone of Influence. Too often, people make it hard by going outside their spheres. They do this to avoid rejection, when in reality your network wants to help you succeed.

Check out your Facebook friend list, your Facebook groups, your favorites on contacts, LinkedIn Connections, former colleagues, past clients, text message lists, people from your church or synagogue, your Twitter followers, and others who fit your ideal customer.

For my Sumo Jerky validation, I wrote down friends who are health conscious, ones who work in an office, and service providers I pay who work in offices.

By the time you've done this you should have filled out at least ten lines, your Dream Ten.

BUT if you're thinking, *Dang, I don't know ten people who can buy this*, then maaaaaaaaybe you should a consider a different business idea. Hoping and praying that a thousand people in the world will magically buy it is living in la-la land, as my father would put it. Go after markets and businesses where you have influence so it's easier to succeed.

Now it's time to turn that list into money!

Scripts for Preselling Your Idea

My buddy Daniel Reifenberger sprung his first successful idea out of his day job at a local Apple store, where he taught baby boomers and little old ladies how to use computers. Every day, his customers would ask him, "Can I just take you home with me?"

He thought the little old ladies were making a pass at him until he realized what they really wanted: in-home technology training.

Daniel was always helping friends and family with their technology, so to validate his in-home tech training idea, he asked them for referrals—and had three paying customers within a week.

He made a profit with his first client doing the work manually and still hasn't spent a dime on his business outside of mileage. His only equipment is a phone and his personal email address.

Today, his technology consulting business is doing $20,000 a MONTH.

Let's take a closer look at the scripts to use and conversations Daniel had.

Validation is a conversation. Not a sales pitch, but a chat to learn about the customer, see if you can help them and if they'll actually pay you.

For this reason, with your Dream Ten, I really recommend you turn the ask into an exploratory conversation, to allow for more learning.

These people really know you and they'll be happy to give you time, so use it to extract what most excites them about your product or not so you can tweak it.

The process to validate your solution with your Dream Ten can be broken down to a three-part framework:

1. Listen
2. Options
3. Transition

First, **Listen.** In this **Listen** step, your job is to get customers talking about their problem.

Here are three questions that will help you in this process:

- What's the most frustrating thing about what's currently going on?
- How would having X make your life better?
- What do you think that X should cost?

Finish with summarizing what the person said. For example, Daniel would say, "So you want an easier way to learn how to use your computer."

> **PRO TIP:** Use what or how questions to encourage a more open dialogue versus why or yes/no questions, which can limit your learning.

It's crucial to really listen and write down their problems, because you're looking for the pain they're feeling and how valuable it would be for them to give you money.

The bigger the pain, the bigger the opportunity!

Next, **Options**. Now that you've uncovered the problem, it's time to suggest options that can solve their problems—and what they'd pay for it. Here are some examples from Daniel:

I'll sell you a digital course on how to fix your computer.

What if I came over and fixed your computer myself?

You're looking for excitement and a willingness to pay. Eye rolls and lower energy from your prospective customer are indicators of low interest.

Now, **Transition**. You know their problem and you know an option to fix it that they are excited about. Now it's time to transition to the sell.

"So you like the idea of me coming over and fixing your computer problem. For $50, I can do it today. Sound good?"

If they pay you, that's Validation success. If you get rejected, I'll show you how to handle that in a moment.

Often you can distill your offer down to three parts: **Price + Benefit + Time.** Strung together, they form an offer sentence. Other examples:

- For $25, I will teach you how to save an hour a day on your Mac, in just twenty minutes.
- For $69, I will teach you how to write better in two hours.
- For $10, I will send you a PDF with ten mind hacks that will change the way you think in ten minutes.
- For $180, I will provide six months of tasty jerky to your office this week.

> **PRO TIP:** Presenting your offer as a comparison can make it easier for your customer to understand. "We are like X but Y." For example, we are like your competitor but twice as cheap. Research shows we better understand the world when something is presented as a contrast with something else.

Asking for Money

There's a big difference between what people say and what people do. Everyone's "interested" until they have to pay.

That's why you don't ask, "Would you be interested?" when you're validating. I've had a lot of people say they're interested and then not pay.

No, you ask for money and ask people to pay immediately.

Now a warning: When you validate, you have to get comfortable with potentially selling a product before you've actually made it. Clearly explain when it will be delivered. Because people are fine with giving you money in advance, as long as you set clear expectations.

Here's my favorite way to ask for money:

"Sign up now while it's still at a discounted price, x percent of y dollars [and you'll be grandfathered in at that price forever]. This offer is only good today."

> **PRO TIP:** Always follow up by sending an email to your first customers asking for feedback. Feedback is a gift you can continually use to improve yourself and your business.

Dealing with Rejection

Of course, success won't always be so immediate when you use direct preselling to validate—in fact, you'll get rejected a whole lot—and this is another instance where the technique shines.

That's because every rejection is an opportunity; you can use it to take a deep dive into customer problems. Remember the **Rejection Goals** from chapter 2. Rejections are TREASURE.

When I get shot down while validating, I have a simple four-question script that flips the *no* into new knowledge, new ideas, and maybe even new customers.

There's a big difference between what people say and what people do. Everyone's "interested" until they have to pay.

1. **"Why not?"** It's really easy to get scared from attacking this one head-on, because what happens if their criticism is right? *But that's exactly what you want to know!*

2. **"Who is one person you know who would really like this?"** Always, always, always ask for a referral! Be specific about what kind of referral and use a number; this makes it highly effective.

3. **"What *would* make this a no-brainer for you?"** If they don't want your product, maybe they'd want something related to it. If they don't want to pay for your dog care app, what about dog walking? A dog hotel? Dog dating?

4. **"What would you pay for that?"** One of the hardest things in a startup is setting prices. Getting potential customers to say what they'd pay is pure gold!

Here's a quick story about how I turned rejection into a sale while validating:

There's a limited-edition movie poster company called Mondo that gets local artists to redesign movie posters and produce a limited number of the reinvented posters for sale.

Mondo tweets when a new poster becomes available and sells out within a few minutes.

So here was my idea: limited-edition posters of tacos from local restaurants!

Instant million-dollar business idea, right? I always consider which color Ferrari I'll buy when I have these ideas!!!

This was going to be easy—Mondo was already doing a similar idea. Plus I knew artists and restaurants would promote the taco posters to their fan base, and within minutes everything would be sold out.

You can probably see where this is going . . .

Then I reached out to some good friends who I KNOW

love tacos and pitched them the idea of a taco poster for $25. The responses I got . . .

- "Uh, so you want me to buy a print for $25 of a . . . taco? I'll pass."
- "Yeah, not my thing, Noah."
- "No one loves tacos as much as you do."

Obviously, I was disappointed not even my close friends would buy a limited-edition taco print. Every time I got rejected, I'd ask the person my four questions.

1. Why not?
2. Who is one person you know who would really like this?
3. What would make this a no-brainer for you?
4. What would you pay for *that*?

The answers, in order, were things like:

- "Because I don't want a taco poster."
- "No one."
- "Well . . . I DO like that taco shirt you have. I'd be interested in that. Like, what does a shirt like that cost? Twenty dollars? Thirty?"

That was the one thing that kept coming up: a specific taco shirt of mine that always got me an insane amount of attention from everyone.

Time for Validation experiment numero dos. I texted the same friends and called others and asked, "You know that taco shirt I wear? Would you want one?"

Here are the responses I got:

- "HELL YEAH. Hook it up."
- "GIMME NOW!"
- "Show me the TACOS!"

Next, I posted a picture of me in the shirt on Facebook and posted a price of $25 per shirt.

After I got fifteen orders via PayPal—no e-commerce, no website; people just sent me the money—I closed off sales and started looking for a manufacturer.

And the Taco Shirt was born. Did it become a big, splashy business? No.

The big takeaway is this: Almost every business idea is guaranteed to fail on the first try. Instagram started as a

It's taco time!

bourbon app. Slack started as a gaming app. Keep validating. Turn rejection into improvements. Feedback is gold.

Keep talking and listening to your customers so you can find out what they need.

> **PRO TIP:** Active communications—calls and texts—work a lot better than passive ones, like posting on Facebook or Twitter and waiting for replies. Try to Direct Message (DM) people, or whatever enables you to get the fastest response time possible.

2. Marketplaces

A classic way to validate your product is to use marketplaces—sites like Facebook Marketplace, Craigslist, Reddit, or whatever you have locally. The great thing about a marketplace is you have a shit-ton of people who are looking to spend money. It's a reliable way to validate different business ideas you're thinking of.

Example: My good bud Neville wanted to validate whether people would pay to rent expensive cameras. He posted one for rent on Craigslist and was able to get $75 for it in a few hours.

The ad Neville posted on Craigslist

This simple Validation cost him $0.00 and a few minutes of time. This is SO much better versus building a website, figuring out a domain, designing a logo, trying to find customers, etc. I also often use a simple "virtual product" process on marketplace sites to test products that don't even exist yet! I find an item similar to the one I want to validate, or I draw up a quick and dirty design of what I want to sell, and then I post it to the marketplace, along with a price, to see if there's an audience.

I love playing disc golf, and once I found this really cool disc on the Reddit DIY channel. So I took the photo of the disc and just posted it on Facebook Marketplace and Twitter with a sentence saying, "Hey, Disc-Golf or Nintendo lovers. I am going to make 5 custom Nintendo discs. If you want one, paypal me $20."

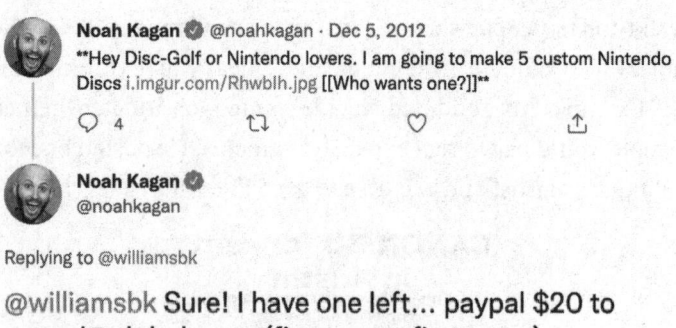

The point is, I didn't try to find a manufacturer. I didn't make a website. I didn't try to test the disc. I just said, "Will anyone actually give me money for this?" And people did. I sold twenty of them and got an online manufacturer to make them and shipped them to customers.

Another good technique involves posting on social media where you have an audience of people.

My assistant Jamie was looking to develop a side hustle, so I asked her if she had ever trained other people to be an assistant because (1) she already had the skill and was very good at it and (2) a lot of other people wanted jobs like hers.

So she posted a message on Facebook right then: "Hey, I'm an assistant. I make a lot of money doing it. I want to help. If you're curious how I do it, I'm happy to help a few other people out. Just leave a comment or message me."

Authentic, straightforward, open, and approachable.

Soon enough, people started responding, and soon she was charging $100 for people to shadow her as she did her job.

That is exactly how you do it!

3. Landing Pages

One really popular approach is to set up a simple landing page using a cheap or free service. Currently Instapage, Unbounce, and ClickFunnels are popular landing page tools. Find the latest landing page tools at MillionDollarWeekend.com.

Then they run a bunch of ads to send people to the site and see if people actually will enter an email address to get on the mailing list, or even preorder the product.

The reason I don't love this approach is you have to spend time setting it up and buying ads, and when you buy ads, you have to become an ad expert. The whole experience is slow and costly. Two things I hate.

My recommendation for you is if you feel you have to do

this, limit your work to forty-eight hours so you won't spend a bunch of time fruitlessly playing with your ads and landing pages or wasting money.

As an example of how to do a landing page right, take what my former intern Justin Mares did while validating what would become the successful bone broth company Kettle & Fire.

To start, he bought the domain bonebroths.com for $12 and set up a basic landing page using Unbounce.

Justin paid around $5 on Fiverr to come up with the simple logo.

After setting up the page and writing the copy, he picked a price. He decided he could make a profit if he charged $29.99 for 16 ounces. If people were willing to give a stranger nearly $30 for a pint of a product they'd never tasted or even seen, then it was probably destined for success.

At the site, people who hit "Order Now" got sent to a PayPal checkout, where they were asked to send money to Justin's email address for "Beef Marrow Bone Broth."

100% Grass-Fed Bone Broth

Get the many health benefits of bone broths without the hassle of making your own! Our bone broth is made with bones from grass-fed, pasture-raised cows and all organic vegetables.

Order Bone Broth Now!

Over 1000 orders placed this month alone!

Heals a Leaky Gut
The gelatin in bone broth protects and heals the lining of the digestive tract, promoting better digestive health.

Absurdly Convenient
Our bone broth is fresh and never frozen, so you get all the benefits of bone broth hassle free. No more dealing with frozen bone broth!

Authentic Bone Broth
Our bone broth is simmered for 24+ hours, only uses organic ingredients and gels in the fridge so you know it's authentic!

The site was ugly enough to give graphic designers the cold sweats. But after Justin bought about $50 of Bing ads, people started actually coming to the site and PayPal-ing him money!

Over the course of the two-week test, he netted almost $500 in revenue. And now Kettle & Fire is a $100 million company—selling broth?!?!

VALIDATED!

The key is: **If you go this route, don't overthink the design, the name, the language, the ads, or any of that. Just focus on seeing if you can get people to buy your product!**

CHALLENGE

Validation.

Your challenge is to get at least three paying customers within forty-eight hours.

Grab your Dream Ten list that you made earlier.

Text, call, direct message, or email—the more real time, the better!

Example script to copy:

YOU: Hey—I remember you really liked beef jerky.

POTENTIAL BUYER: Yeah, eat it all the time.

YOU: Awesome! I'm working on a new project with healthy beef jerky. Think you'll love it. You down to be my first customer, only $20 a month.

POTENTIAL BUYER: I don't know, what kind of jerky?

YOU: Healthy, sourced by me, and if you don't like it, happy to refund you.

POTENTIAL BUYER: Sounds good. Can I pay later?

YOU: Why don't you Venmo, PayPal, or send me cash now so I can confirm you. Only taking ten orders as part of the first batch.

POTENTIAL BUYER: Money sent.

After you've validated, if no one is buying, choose another idea and start over. Head back to chapter 3 and begin again!

If you've validated your idea with at least three customers, that's AMAZING! YOU DID IT, my friend! YOU HAVE A BUSINESS! Boom! Now, let's talk about how to grow your business.

> **Free Bonus:** Grab my six ways to enhance your offering at MillionDollarWeekend.com.

PART 3

Grow It

Make Money While You Sleep

YOU MADE IT HAPPEN. I'M PROUD OF YOU!

Let's begin creating the growth machine to turn your first customers into a community of fans that will drive your business's success. I'm going to show you the exact marketing strategy I've used with every one of my businesses. In the following chapters, you'll learn:

- **Social Media Is for Growth . . .** How to create your inner circle of a hundred true fans (shout-out, Kevin Kelly, for the inspiration) in thirty days, choose the right platform for you, and keep it growing with your unfair advantage.
- **. . . Email Is for Profit.** How to lead this audience into your ATM—your email list—so that you can convert them from an audience to customers.

- **The Growth Machine.** How to set up your marketing experiments and double down on what's working.
- **52 Chances This Year.** How to convert your dream life to daily actions.

CHAPTER 6

Social Media Is for Growth . . .

Build an Audience
Who Will Support You for Life

After my father died, I began dreaming of Bo Jackson. The only athlete in history to be both an NFL and an MLB all-star, he was one of the most popular athletes on the planet during the early nineties.

I remember how much adoration my father felt for Bo. Coming from nothing, Bo was a shy and stuttering Alabamian who had achieved all the fame and riches imaginable, and my father came to see Bo's success as proof of the American Dream. They also were both named Bo.

Maybe it was out of a desire to pay my respects, or maybe it was just to feel close to him again, but when my dad passed away a few years ago, I knew one thing: I had to meet Bo. The thing was, he had disappeared from the limelight.

He wasn't working in Hollywood and he wasn't using an agent to keep his fame alive. He was just living a quiet life in Chicago. As I was trying to contact Bo, I learned that in 2012 he had started Bo Bikes Bama, an annual charity bike ride to raise money for emergency disaster relief in Alabama.

That's when I decided the best thing I could do was offer my help. This was a great cause, and if I helped him, maybe he'd meet with me and come on the podcast. So I turned to my audience, which I built through years of free YouTube videos and weekly email newsletters and Q&As. I asked them and was shocked by the reaction.

This was the message I sent out to my audience:

> When I was growing up, my father's favorite athlete was Bo Jackson. And today, Bo needs our help.
>
> My father isn't alive to help, but we can!
>
> Every year, Bo does a bike ride to raise money for emergency disaster relief in Alabama. This year, **my goal is to raise $25,000 to help the children and state of Alabama.**
>
> Donate to Bo Bikes Bama using the form below. Fundraising ends March 31st. **I'm matching 1-1 up to $5,000.**
>
> **GIFT LEVELS**
> - **Amigo—$10**—Letter. I'll personally mail you a thank-you letter from Alabama.
> - **Homie—$50**—Custom deck of cards. I'll mail you a custom deck of playing cards with each card designed by my favorite artist.
> - **Sidekick—$100**—Cards + shirt. Custom deck of cards and Taco Powered T-shirt.
> - ***NEW* Hermano**—$500—Phone call. Everything above and a one-hour consult with Noah.
> - **Inner Circle—$1,000**—Everything above and Austin bike ride. Go on a bike ride and hang out with me in Austin. Plus a Minaal backpack, and clothes from Rhone and Huckberry.
> - **BFF—$10,000**—Mexico City. Let's do a taco and talk business at a Michelin-starred restaurant in Mexico City. All expenses paid.

In three days we raised $30,000 from my audience in small donations, all without going viral. Two days later, Bo called me personally to thank me, and soon thereafter he appeared on my podcast.

"Of course you were able to raise such a crazy amount," I hear you responding, my dear reader. "You have a huge audience!" But here's the remarkable thing: when I went down the list of 102 names of people who donated to Bo Bikes Bama, I recognized nearly every name! I had interacted with these people. I'd given them business advice. I occasionally just said, "You're doing great, keep going."

These weren't followers or an anonymous audience. They were what marketing guru Seth Godin calls your "smallest viable audience" or what *Wired* magazine cofounder Kevin Kelly has called "1,000 true fans"—all built by connecting with people whose particular challenges and interests overlapped with my particular skills and passions.

The lifetime value, not to mention the lifelong joy, generated by a community of 100 high-value, attentive fans who know, like, and trust you will dwarf whatever short-term satisfaction you may get from having 10,000 low-value, inattentive followers. And it doesn't matter if you sell mountain biking gear, cooking lessons, or SEO services—there are hundreds, maybe even thousands, of people among the billions of internet users that will not only pay for what you're selling now but will follow and support your every entrepreneurial move for years to come.

A community who already knows you, who follows you, who is rooting for you is one of the most powerful forces in business, and it's created through generosity. Adding value without expectation. Helping them with their journey without asking for an immediate return. Sometimes it's helping them by boosting their self-esteem with a simple compliment.

I've spent twenty years giving out free content to people through OkDork and AppSumo. So when I finally said, "Hey, I'm raising money for charity. Do you guys want to contribute?" it was easy for me to ask, and saying yes was a no-brainer for my community. It takes time to build a real audience.

Back in 2000, I started OkDork.com to document my journey for friends from high school and college. In those early years, posts were all over the place—marketing, pictures of my stuffed frog Seymour, things happening in college. As my blog evolved, it became more focused on marketing and starting a business based on my interests and requests from readers.

The network of people who helped make my success possible were built by putting myself out there, building my businesses in public, failures and all. For instance, Seth Godin responded to one of my blog posts, enabling me to meet him (my marketing idol). And I got the Mint job because of building in public.

Name drop alert: Because I kept putting myself out there, I also met Tim Ferriss, Andrew Chen, Mike Posner, Bo Jackson, James Clear, Ryan Holiday, Firefox co-creator Blake Ross, bestselling author Ramit Sethi, and even my coauthor, Tahl Raz. Meeting people like this is one of the best things in life.

Now, I've never deliberately "built a personal brand." I was always just myself. I liked sharing. I was honest and transparent. **People get hooked on CHARACTERS. People do business with REAL PEOPLE. Especially those who feel like a friend.**

Take Danny Wang Design, the local lawn care company that posts riveting weekly 45-second before-and-after clips of beautifying their clients' yards to snappy music (and targets their posts to homeowners within their service area). They now have 2.3 million TikTok followers and regularly get 150,000 views—and often TONS more—for their backyard #transformations. And Danny himself is nowhere to be found in the videos.

Finding Your Unique Angle

So how do you find your unique angle to start building up your community?

When people come to me asking how I can get my newsletter or blog posts or tweets to stand out from the crowd, our conversation almost always centers around getting them to understand how their special sauce is the **unfair advantage** that will make them shine.

Take, for example, Ben Kenyon. Ben is the head strength and conditioning coach for the Philadelphia 76ers NBA basketball team. He's also CEO and founder of Great Day Squad. He's a great guy. Super strong. Funny. Amazing beard.

Look at that beard!

I had the luck to interview him for OkDork because he wanted my advice on starting a newsletter. He thought his problem was that he didn't know the process. But the mechanics come down to figuring out how to embrace and amplify your uniqueness in a way that attracts people to become friends and customers.

I asked him one question:

"What's your unique angle in thirty seconds or less?" In other words, why would anyone care to read his newsletter?

I know that sounds harsh, but that's the first question you have to answer before you put yourself into the public sphere.

Pressed into defining his unique angle, Ben paused. He rumpled his face up, laughed nervously, and shrugged. This is hard!

Finally he spoke, slowly, and then with confidence.

Listen to how Ben defined his angle, his sauce:

"I've been a performance coach for the last fourteen years, working with the best athletes in the world. Helping people perform better is my groove. I want to help anybody who wants to have a great day and shift them into the mentality to dominate their life. I have information to share when it comes to dealing with the best."

That is beautiful! Both in its heartfelt honesty and authenticity, but also in its clarity.

Let's pick it apart and look at what he did in those four sentences:

1. He defines who he is,
2. Why you should trust him,
3. What he is passionate about, and
4. What unique thing this prepares him to do for you.

It is clear, approachable, direct, and short. The first three sentences define what makes him special (fourteen years helping the best athletes in the world perform better!), and the fourth (how he's solving his customers' problems, teaching mindsets needed to dominate life) defines the kind of love and attention he'll generously dispense to cultivate a community.

Take a minute, and as Ben has done, write out a pitch in your journal describing your special sauce.

CHALLENGE

Write out your unique angle.

There are no right answers here. You can change these any time you'd like.

1. Who are you?
   _____

2. Why should people listen?
   _____

3. What are you passionate about?
   _____

4. What will you do for people?
   _____

Pick a Platform

With your unique angle, you need to reach an audience, and the best way to do it for FREE is through social media.

You can choose any FREE platform:

- Photographers love Instagram to showcase their newest cool stuff to the world.
- Consultants love to stand on a soapbox at LinkedIn.
- Journalists, marketers, and others like the few hundred characters of Twitter.
- Designers can show off their work at Dribble.
- Authors can start a blog for free on WordPress.com.

And that's just today. The platforms are going to change. But what won't change is how you pick one. You need to know three things to choose:

1. Which site has the audience you want to connect with?
2. What medium do YOU enjoy creating content in?
3. What disproportionate results will you get compared to the work you put in?

So you can see how this process works for a real person, let's break down how I chose my platform. To start, I eliminated the ones that *don't* work for me.

- **Instagram**: I don't take a lot of pics. Bye-bye, Insta. But hey, if you're an interior designer like Kelsey Hutchins, where are people going to look for photos of your work? Instagram, without a doubt. That's how she gets most of her business.

- **Podcasting**: I tried it for years, and frankly the audience is HIGHLY engaged, but growing that audience relative to the work involved was near impossible. No matter what I did, I couldn't grow it. A limited number of people listen to podcasts, and currently, discovering new podcasts is nearly impossible. However, Jordan Harbinger has turned his love of interviewing and podcasts into a seven-figure business: *The Jordan Harbinger Show*.

- **LinkedIn**: Great audience of businesspeople, but it's incredibly noisy, and going viral on it is really tough. But Justin Welsh has used LinkedIn to sell a course that brought in $1.3 million in the first two years.

- **Blogging**: I love blogging on OkDork and still do it, but the volume of Google searches has gone down overall for me. The work of posting doesn't drive as many viral shares anymore because more of the audience is spending their time directly on social media. Former *Rolling Stone* writer Matt Taibbi brings in 1.3 million visitors a month and over $500,000 a year on Substack, so blogging can still work.

- **Twitter**: I love it, but the audience isn't growing—their monthly users have been flat for years. Going viral works there, but getting people off the platform and buying on yours is tough. Nick Huber of The Sweaty Startup has turned his storage business into an even larger business mostly from tweeting provocative comments about how to run companies.

- **TikTok**: No shade on TikTok here, but in my experience—1 million followers there or 100,000 on YouTube? Not equivalent. I'd take YouTube every time. In fact, by one measure, 1 YouTube sub equals 25 on TikTok! Then again... if your audience is all under twenty-five and getting all its news, dance moves, and buying advice on TikTok, you've got to go where your people are. I've started experimenting with TikTok and have gotten 150,000-plus followers repurposing my YouTube content but no direct business impact after multiple attempts.

Just cause these platforms don't work for me does not mean they won't work for you. The MORE important part is to start with just one as an experiment.

For me it was . . . YouTube!

Oh, yeah, come to Papa. YouTube is the LARGEST STREAMING VIDEO SITE ON THE INTERNET. It has 122 million active daily users who consume a billion hours of video each day. PLUS, YouTube monetizes your videos for you with ads and hosts them at no cost (my favorite price).

YouTube is simply the best way I've ever seen to grow an audience—and an audience of quality—for free.

The challenge with YouTube is that it's harder to create a video than write a tweet, which discourages most people. However, I see that as an advantage since it means less competition if you're willing to do it.

Or maybe you hate being on camera. But that's no excuse, either. SO many channels have gotten massive like SunnyV2 (two plus million subscribers to his documentaries about famous people), and we've never seen his face.

You also don't need an expensive studio or Hollywood gear. I started my 750,000-plus subscriber channel shirtless in my living room talking about marketing, shooting with my iPhone 12. Nothing fancy needed.

No excuses. Just get to it.

The key principle is to start right now to build your audience and then move them to your email list (which we'll cover in the next chapter).

The internet gives ANYONE the chance to have the same broadcasting power as a massive media brand. No permission is needed to build your own audience.

> **CHALLENGE**
>
> **Update your bio.**
>
> Choose your one platform, and using the unique angle pitch you wrote out before, clean up and rewrite your profile/bio on that platform to reflect who you are and how you help your ideal customer.
>
> _____
>
> _____
>
> _____
>
> **Here's my bio:** Chief Sumo at @AppSumo. #30 at Facebook. Helping entrepreneurs at Okdork.com.

Creating Content for Your Core Circle

In the time it will take for you to read this sentence, the content on my blog (okdork.com), Twitter (@noahkagan) and YouTube (youtube.com/okdork) will have reached an extra 5,000 people FOR FREE. That's wild, amazing, and doable for you, too. A good post or video works while you sleep without any additional cost.

The internet gives ANYONE the chance to have the same broadcasting power as a massive media brand. **No permission is needed to build your own audience.**

Take Ali Abdaal. In 2017 he was a Cambridge University medical student who thought he'd try his hand at YouTube.

His videos included things like tips on studying and memorization for the BMAT. This is the British medical school entrance exam, the BioMedical Admissions Test.

He made videos about how to take Section 1 of the exam and

then about how to take Section 2. Later he showed how to prep for the med school interview. And his audience grew because there was a very specific group of people who were desperate for Ali's expertise on a very specific problem they faced.

Today, Ali is a massive star with more than 4.4 million YouTube subscribers and earns more than $400,000 a month.

Ali is one of the guys I respect most on YouTube and a great guide for the audience-gathering journey, so let's unpack his playbook for all of us to replicate!

Ali uses what I call the **Content Circle Framework**. The basic idea is to start with specific topics for a tiny circle to build raving fans, then slowly expand your circle of content to influence larger groups of people.

Here are the three steps:

1. **Core Circle:** Start with a very narrow audience. Ali started with the medical school exams for British people. Your niche within a niche can be the most obscure thing imaginable, as long as it makes you and your audience passionate.
2. **Medium Circle:** As you move bigger, your content should overlap somewhat with what concerns your Core Circle, but it should appeal to a broader audience. Ali started talking about studying and productivity in general, since that's required for all students.
3. **Large Circle:** Here you go for the largest audience possible that's still related. Some of Ali's most watched videos are about his salary—made possible by his medical video fame—or the latest Apple product—which he uses to increase productivity. All the circles should still include your core audience but keep expanding your circle of influence.

Here are examples of other people who followed the **Content Circle Framework**:

Dustin Wunderlich of Dustin's Fish Tanks started by literally reviewing fish tanks. And you know what? There's a real audience for that. As time went on, he expanded to all things fish, like what kind of fish to buy to rid your tank of algae and what the top aquarium plants are, and now he has 150,000 subscribers and a million-dollar online business selling fish and aquarium supplies.

Then there's Kyle Lasota, the Austin-based creator behind the very cool YouTube channel kylegotcamera. Kyle's into biohacking—he reviews cold plunges, red light therapy, saunas, sleep gadgets, supplements, and all that. While he's got a modest audience—16,000 subscribers on YouTube—he's built such a tight community with his core that even though a lot of his videos get only 400 views, he nets a cool $1 million a year from affiliate sales. He knows his Core Circle and they LOVE him!

Or take an offline example: Andy Schneider, aka the Chicken Whisperer, just loved raising chickens in his backyard outside Atlanta. People kept asking him for info and hints on raising their own, so he started holding regular meetings about raising backyard poultry (like real-life YouTube!). Five years later, Schneider had a radio show, a magazine, and a book, and now he travels around the United States, leading workshops. Hundreds of thousands of dollars followed. But it all started with serving a niche within a niche—backyard farmers who wanted to raise chickens.

To get started, identify a value that a specific group of people—your Core Circle—want and become a reliable source of information for them. Here's a formula you can use—**outcome you'll deliver + target market**.

Here's an example of Content Circles for a housecleaning company:

- **Core Circle:** How to clean your evaporative cooler + in the Southwest USA.
- **Medium Circle:** How to choose laundry detergents + for new homeowners.
- **Large Circle:** The ten best vacuums + for a family.

Once you have your outcome and market figured, you need to find a unique viewpoint in your niche.

To come up with your unique viewpoint, ask yourself a few questions:

- What is something everyone thinks is true—but you think is wrong?
- What is something nobody in your target market is talking about—but should be?
- What are the biggest mistakes people in your market are making—but are totally blind to?

Ultimately, your audience wants to learn something from you that's relevant, useful, and surprising. And they want to do that by going on a journey with you.

CHALLENGE

Create your own Content Circle.

Think back to your validation days. Who are the customers you want to appeal to and what's the outcome you can create content for? What's the unique point of view in your content they'd be excited to hear about?

> **Formula = Outcome you'll deliver + the target market**
>
> **Core Circle:**
> _____
>
> **Medium Circle:**
> _____
>
> **Large Circle:**
> _____

Be the Guide, Not the Guru

If I've learned anything from the thousands of videos I have created for YouTube, it is that **people don't want to be lectured at by an all-knowing guru—they want to tag along with a guide**. That's why I post so many videos where I reveal the nuts and bolts of my processes.

Ali is an absolute genius at this process. His videos—which are almost always titled "How I . . ." rather than "How to . . ."—follow him as he guides viewers through how he studies for medical school entrance exams or takes notes on his iPad Pro, or how he learned to type really fast.

The goal here is to document what YOU do, not what you think everyone else should do. When you position yourself as someone who is on a journey and document your process and your progress, you become relatable, and that is what audiences long for. Some of my most popular videos feature me failing, often. It's fascinating that people want to see what's really going on, not the highlight reel we think they want.

If you think you don't have anything worth documenting,

you're probably wrong. Whether you have a desk job or some unique hobby, there is something about your process that others can learn from.

An example of this is the Matt's Off-Road Recovery YouTube channel, which has 1.4 million subscribers showing Matt just doing his regular day job—using his tow truck to help people who've gotten stuck—in a way that makes it entertaining and instructive.

The cool thing with becoming your audience's guide is it makes them want to interact with you.

That's why I regularly co-create with my audience by doing the business equivalent of schoolyard dares. Like when I dared my Monthly1K class to supply me with a business idea to validate, which became Sumo Jerky. I ask my audience to challenge me to do something difficult; then I go out and do it.

Getting your audience involved helps them feel like an integral part of the show, which boosts the chances they'll engage with your videos, which pushes your content up the rankings—and attracts even more subscribers.

Devin Stone of LegalEagle is a genius at this way of building audience engagement—in his push to help people "think like a lawyer," he encourages his audience to leave comments in the form of objections, which he then sustains or overrules in the comment thread.

CHALLENGE

Post one piece of content.

Now it's time to post content publicly.

Now, this piece of content can come in any format. You know I LOVE me some YouTube, but as you've seen, different niches work on different platforms. The content you create can be a YouTube video, a Twitter thread, or a blog post. You've already taken the first steps in this chapter.

1. **Your Unique Angle**—the secret sauce nobody else has
2. **The Platform** you're going to post on
3. **Your Content Circle**—the narrow audience who you'll laser-target
4. **Posting it TODAY**

This last step is obviously the hardest one. Don't worry about scripts, camera equipment, or even if it gets any views. The important part is taking the first step at building your community.

Next, we're going to show you how to turn the community into customers with an email list.

CHAPTER 7

... Email Is for Profit

Use Email to Make a F*&k-Ton of Money

AppSumo's first $10,000 day started with an email about a boner.

I was just starting to build AppSumo, and my whole business was based on sending emails to subscribers and presenting them with an awesome deal.

Up to that point, the emails were written by me and a seventeen-year-old Bulgarian guy named Nikola who didn't speak English very well (no offense, Nikola), and we were making around $100 per email. Our most profitable email to date had made $1,000. I was right where you are now—just starting out.

And then my friend Neville Medhora started bugging me to let him write one of our emails.

Neville, a copywriter, was convinced that AppSumo's emails were being ignored because they were always "SELLING SELLING SELLING." Entrepreneurs who expressed an attractive story made more sales, he said.

But I was skeptical of the "magic" of story. My emails were fine; I was targeting the right people; AppSumo would grow.

Still, I figured I had nothing to lose from giving him a chance, so I let Neville draft the email for our next offer—an app called Kernest that helped with fonts, a subject I know nothing about.

Normally, Nikola would have just written: "There's a deal on this product and you get to save $1,000!" Throw in a buy button and that was my typical email. It was just "Go buy!"—not much more than that.

An hour later Neville sent me a rough draft of an email, and what he wrote completely changed my mind about how entrepreneurs should interact with their customers.

It started with a line I will never forget:

"If you get a boner when I whisper the word 'Garamond' into your ear . . . you might be interested."

I had no idea what Garamond was, but from that line on, the email grew increasingly entertaining and captivating. It showed people that I'd had a funny struggle with fonts and it taught them how they could overcome it with Kernest.

Neville told a long story about how Steve Jobs was fascinated by fonts—specifically, about how he loved the font Helvetica and made sweet, sweet love to it. It was a silly story—but it brought the reader into my head.

The actual monetary offer wasn't any better than the offers I put in my earlier emails. The big difference was the copy. It was an authentic person on the page, struggling, telling jokes, laughing, and teaching.

And . . .

My email list loved the new me.

We made $9,563 in profit in twenty-four hours! By putting

personality into the email, we made nearly a hundred times more money!

Here's the final email we sent out (we had to take the "boner" out—corporate email obscenity filters and all):

SUBJECT: Steve Jobs was originally obsessed with typography
TO: <testy3@okdork.com>
FROM: AppSumo <noah@appsumo.com>

I'm going to save you a bunch of time

If the names "Lucida Sans Unicode" or "Courier New" don't mean anything to you, go ahead and close this message.

You see, my friend, today we're reaching out only to the community of people known as font fanatics.

You know who you are!

If your knees go weak when I whisper, "GARAMOND."

... you might be one of 'em.

You can call yourself a designer or a developer to normal society, but behind closed doors we know the elegance of Verdana's curves turn you on ... and that's why we're here today.

As Steve Jobs described his obsession with beautiful typography:

"I learned about Serif and Sans Serif typefaces. About varying the amount of space between different letter combinations. About what makes great typography great. It was beautiful, historical, artistically subtle in a way science can't capture ... and I found it fascinating." Steve Jobs

If, like Jobs, your lust for fonts craves more and more every month, the solution stands before you:

Kernest.

Did you hear that? I said: KERNEST.

It takes an obsessive eye to pick which fonts play well together, and every month a new combination of fonts is delivered to you . . . complete with HTML and CSS highlighting.

Maybe you're like me:

You can easily tell when something "looks really good" . . . but you sometimes don't know WHY.

This is a problem I have. I can see a "clean-looking" web page, but can't tell why my Franken-site doesn't look as slick. Often the answer is typography. When I smash Arial 12 with Tahoma 36, it somehow doesn't work . . . and don't even get me started on the color schemes . . .

Once again, Kernest to the rescue.

When you get your new fonts, you can rejoice that you don't have to fool around with them. . . . They are ready to implement, and the grueling process of marrying fonts together has been taken care of by the Almighty Kernest himself.

Most things in life aren't free, and don't dare expect Kernest to be.

Kernest charges $15/month for delivering the most obsessively picked font combinations every month. This, my dear Sumo-ling, is . . .

$180/year.

A fair price for making your clients knees quiver when they see your stunning work.

But full price makes the AppSumo angry (and hungry).

We have konvinced Kernest (through intimidation and force) to give away a lifetime membership at less than the yearly price.

This means no monthly payments, no yearly payments, no alimony payments, no NOTHING for life. Just magical font combinations every month capable of making an ugly project come to life from beautiful typography.

As you know from past AppSumo promotions, we always get late-to-the-gamers whining and pleading to let them buy the deal after it's over.

The countdown timer on AppSumo does not lie.

If you are a designer, take action NOW to stand out from lifeless design and stay ahead of the game. Get your lifetime membership to Kernest here:

KERNEST.

PS: We also convinced (aka threatened) Kernest to give away the last FOUR months of font combinations for every lifetime signup through this deal. You get them soon as you sign up.

Only 48 hours left.

Your Pal,
@NoahKagan

All it took was a bad joke and a hundred times increase in revenue to make me rethink how I communicated with my email list. The email was FUN. It wasn't pure utility. Sales have repeatedly been shown to go UP when the people selling are enjoying themselves.

Over the fifteen years before I launched AppSumo, I had learned how to grow a pretty huge audience at OkDork by promoting interesting people, exposing my passions, interacting with my followers, and just all in all having fun being myself.

Somewhere along the way, though, I came to believe that the audience-building, excitable nerd me and the business me had to be separate.

Until this $10,000 profit eye-opener I had failed to apply my audience-building powers to my businesses. Every time I launched a new product or business, I started building anew from the ground up.

Like I had amnesia.

Neville's email changed all of that. It gave me permission to make who I am a part of how I market and sell.

More important, it opened my eyes to the singular power of email. I now could see how social media, telling stories, and email could create a really large business.

In chapter 6, you built an audience on social media for FREE, and you learned how to appeal to them with the generosity that will lead them to root for your success. Now you're going to lead this audience into your own ATM—your email list—so that you are in regular personal contact with them and can convert them from an audience to customers. I'm going to show a simple four-step process to turn your audience into a massive paycheck—which is what a vibrant and engaged email subscriber list is.

Ready? Let's go!

In this chapter, you'll learn:

- How to use a piece of useful free content to get people excited to sign up for your list.
- How to create a simple, effective landing page and publicize it far and wide.
- How to automate your email system so it's sending out emails to new subscribers twenty-four hours a day.

Your Email List Is Power

Which of these options is the most valuable for your business?

A. 100 email subscribers

B. 1,000 YouTube subscribers

C. 10,000 Instagram followers

Email is the king and queen of communicating with customers.

The answer may surprise you, but it's A. **Email is the king and queen of communicating with customers.**

Email is the most valuable channel because it allows you to own the distribution and the communication with your customers, and not be at the mercy of another platform's fickle algorithm.

Still skeptical? Let me give you six reasons why email is the best:

1. My company AppSumo generates $65 million a year in total transactions. And you know what? Nearly 50 percent of that comes from email. This percentage has been consistent for more than ten years.

2. Don't believe me? I have 120,000 Twitter followers, 750,000 YouTube subscribers, and 150,000 TikTok fans—and I would give them all up for my 100,000 email subscribers. Why? Every time I send an email, 40,000 people open it and consume my content. I'm not hoping the platform gods will allow me to reach them. On the other platforms, anywhere between 100 and 1 million people pay attention to my content, but it's not consistent or in my control.

3. I know what you're saying: "C'mon, Noah, email is dead." Now ask yourself, when was the last time you checked your email? Exactly. Email is used obsessively by over 4 billion people! It's the largest way of communicating at scale that exists today. Eighty-nine percent of people check it EVERY DAY!

4. Social media decides who and how many people you're seen by. One tweak to the algorithm, and you're toast. Remember the digital publisher LittleThings? Yeah, no one else does, either. They closed after they lost 75 percent of their 20,000,000 monthly visitors when Facebook changed

its algorithm in 2018. CEO Joe Speiser says it killed his business and he lost $100 million.

5. You own your email list. Forever. If AppSumo shuts down tomorrow, my insurance policy, my sweet sweet baby, my beloved, my email list comes with me and makes anything I do after so much easier. Because it's mine.

6. It also doesn't cost you significant money to grow your list or to communicate with your list, whereas Facebook or Google ads consistently cost money.

Honestly, the number one regret of just about every entrepreneur I know is this: "I wish I started my email list sooner." Don't be that person. Email marketing needs to be your new best friend.

The only way to consistently monetize whatever audience you build, wherever you build it, is with email. That means that you're not really "building an audience" if you don't have their email. No matter how many new social media platforms pop up, email is still the most powerful channel for deepening your relationship with your audience.

Even if you don't have a business at this very moment, it's great to start building your email list NOW—so when you *do* want to have a business, you already have a trusted group of people who WANT to help you out.

There is one vitally important point I want to make before we move on. That is, the importance of having a list of people who want you to win. Sheer size is not the metric to use to evaluate an email list. It doesn't matter if you have 100,000 subs if none of them care about you.

One of the very first clients of my great friend Charlie Hoehn (he's worked for Tim Ferriss, Ramit Sethi, Tucker Max) was a real estate mogul who bought an email list of 1 million subscribers to promote his book. The list was made up of people who'd signed up for discounts at retail and restaurant chains—and had nothing whatsoever to do with the mogul. Charlie emailed them a sequence of five emails, AND FEWER THAN 100 PEOPLE OPENED THE MESSAGES. It's about quality, not quantity.

What percentage of your list opens every email because they feel like they know and trust you? **A healthy email list has a 20 percent open rate. Target that.**

Having a bond that leads people to open your emails—not the size of the list—is where the power of email lies.

The BIG question now is, how can you get your first subscribers? Let me show you.

Set Up a Landing Page

Your audience needs somewhere to go to actually join your email list. Even though you can technically start an email list just by emailing people in Gmail or your local email client . . . just saying. The way companies, marketers, entrepreneurs, and content creators do this is by sending their audiences to a landing page.

Julien Marion, a Monthly1K student, did a landing page for his business Sleep Sumo, helping people sleep better.

That's it! Give me your email, and I'll give you a bonus resource: one free tip each week to improve your sleep. Simple.

A landing page is a simple web page with an image, a few words, and a box where people can input their email address to get future updates. This is where you can offer them the bonus content, aka Lead Magnet (see the next page), you just created.

All you need your website to do is to communicate a value proposition and provide a way to capture emails.

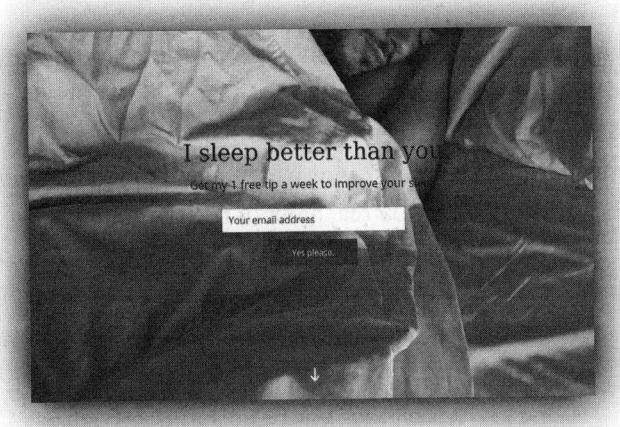

Julien's Sleep Sumo landing page

> ### CHALLENGE
>
> **Build your landing page.**
>
> You can set up one like Julien's for free with SendFox.com (a service I helped build).
>
> There are also other services like Mailchimp.com, Webflow.com, and ConvertKit.com to create landing pages.
>
> Go to MillionDollarWeekend.com to see more landing page examples.

Getting Your First 100 Email Subscribers

0 to 10—The Dream Ten

What's the easiest way to start building your list? Use your existing network.

Yes, your Dream Ten. These are people who know you and care about you. The members of this highly engaged audience are waiting to visit, subscribe to, and share your website and content. They are your most powerful tool for knocking over that initial subscription domino.

My mom, my brother, and my other close friends are on my mailing list. Always look at what assets and networks you have available before you reach out to randoms.

Here's a template you can use. My former Monthly1K student Bryan Harris used it and he's been able to get to 10,000-plus subscribers at Videofruit. He sent his Dream Ten (and more) a message that says:

Hey [name]!

I just wanted to let you know that I'm starting [description of your new business].

I'm going to publish [one article per week/a weekly tip] on how to [subject].

Is this something you are interested in?

Here's an easy way to sign up! [Insert landing page address] Or you can just write back with "Yes, dude, I'd like to," and I'll do it for you!

Hope things are great!

[Your name]

That's it!

Then, if they respond with a yes—which they most likely will, because you know them—put their email on your subscriber list.

11 to 50—Lazy Marketing

Now that you have a landing page, you've got to publicize it. Obviously you're already doing that by putting it in your calls to action inside your videos, TikToks, or wherever you are promoting yourself online (and in their corresponding descriptions). But you can go a lot further by putting a link to it in every point of contact you have with others.

That means putting the landing page address in your:

- Email signature
- Biography on Twitter, LinkedIn, TikTok, Instagram, and Facebook

Those offer more leverage than most people think.

On average, a person sends *around 40 emails per day*. That means that every day you have a chance to place your new landing page address in at least 40 emails.

That's 40 lottery tickets with above-average chances of winning!

Just make it fun, like this one of mine:

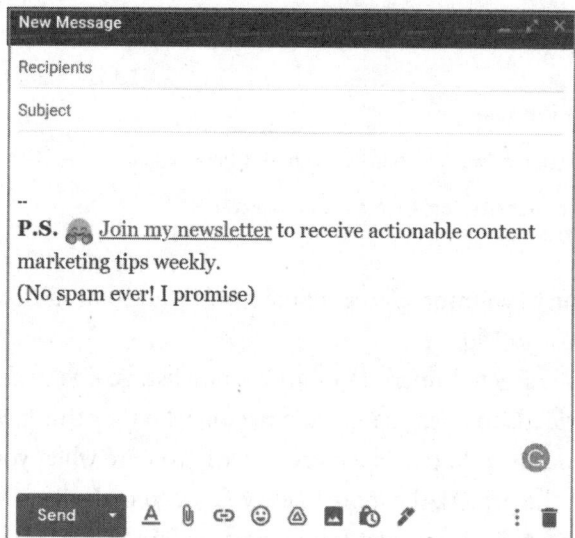

A real email signature I use to grow my email list

(When you add your landing page to your email and your social bios, you can measure the traffic and conversion rate you get from these mentions with Bitly.com or Linktree.com, website address shorteners that track clicks.)

> **CHALLENGE**
>
> **Update email signature and social media bios.**
>
> Put your landing page address in your email signature and your social bios. Send me a link to your new landing page at twitter.com/noahkagan—I'd love to hear from you!

51 to 100—Post in Your Places

You already have a social presence. Now it's time to post a modified version of that email above in Facebook, Snapchat, Twitter, Reddit groups—or wherever you're active.

> Hey Everyone
>
> Starting a "weekly" newsletter about [subject].
>
> Go to website.com to join the newsletter.

Posting in your top places should move your total subscribers list close to 100.

Use targeted referrals to grow your list. Ask your family and friends to refer one specific person who they think would like your newsletter. The more specific you are when you describe the person, the more likely you are to make it easier for them to do it. Take what I did for Sumo Jerky: "Do you know someone who makes purchase decisions at an office—and likes a good laugh?"

Don't forget about people you work with. I know there can be conflict, but you have more friends than you realize who want to support you!

Growing Beyond Your First Subscribers

Chris Von Wilpert was trying to build a content marketing agency. He knew that the marketing software company HubSpot—with the number five top worldwide traffic rank in the online marketing tech space—was a massive object of interest among the marketers who made up his potential client base. So he decided on a strategy:

1. Write an insanely detailed blog post dissecting the success of and drawing lessons from HubSpot's content marketing approach. He spent forty hours working on this.
2. Use social media and pretty much everything else to get that post in front of his ideal customers.
3. Put a call to action (CTA) at the end of the post telling readers to sign up to receive a download of growth hacks he'd put together.

After all of Chris's intense outreach, 5,000 people had viewed his blog post reverse engineering HubSpot's success. And within two weeks, his email list grew from 0 to over 1,000 subscribers! Just putting out a great free piece of content and incentivizing the readers with a Lead Magnet (the free growth hacks spreadsheet for those who signed up) worked!

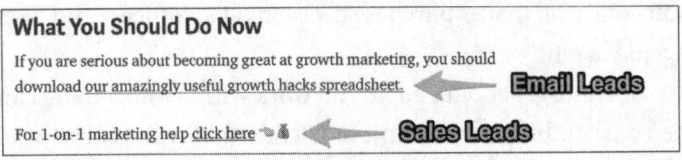

Chris's Lead Magnets

I was one of them. I thought the post and his audience outreach was so fire, I reached out personally:

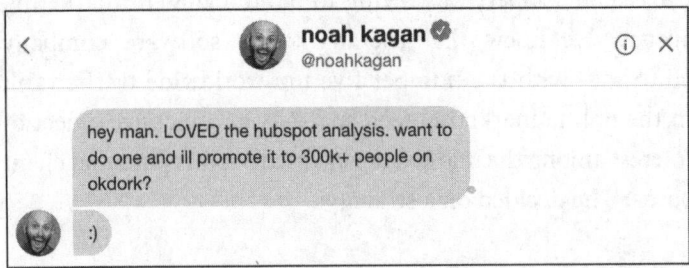

In the end, that turned into a $100,000 payday for Chris, because after I asked him to reverse engineer another company's growth strategy for *my* OkDork and it became my most shared blog post EVER, I offered him $100,000 to live in our Austin offices for six months and execute his content marketing strategy for AppSumo. Seriously!

Using a Lead Magnet gives people an incentive to join your email list vs. just asking people to sign up.

Now, not every Lead Magnet has to involve the complexity and dedication that Chris's did. Plenty of more modest content, combined with attractive bonuses, can seriously boost your email subscriber list.

Here are four examples of Lead Magnets I use:

- A checklist that can be used to properly perform something I explained in a video.

- A template for determining, say, a business's profit margin.
- An advanced guide that goes further into the details of a subject of one of my videos.
- A unique book that provides substantial value but is offered for free. For me, it is *11 Side Hustle Ideas to Make $500/Day from Your Phone*.

The appropriate opt-in incentive depends on your content. Here are other types of examples:

- A DIY carpenter could offer plans to make a corner table.
- A marketing YouTuber could offer scripts of what to say on sales phone calls.
- A landscaping expert might offer recommendations for which kinds of grass to use around the United States.

YouTuber Nick True at Mapped Out Money, who makes video tutorials that teach the best practices for using the personal budgeting software YNAB, found that he gets the highest sign-up rates when he offers a checklist that relates to the video. His followers really like having a resource that they can use to put his advice into practice.

Jess Dante of Love and London runs a YouTube channel helping viewers plan their trips to London by suggesting lesser-known restaurants and stores to visit. Her superstar opt-in incentive is a free *London 101 Guide* with everything a first-time visitor needs to know. It's been downloaded more than 45,000 times.

Where you make your call to action will also have an impact on your success building your email list. You can make your call to action in a variety of places or ways inside your videos.

One of the best ways is to give a short, relevant tease of the bonus or resource you're offering within the YouTube video and tell people where they can learn more.

> **CHALLENGE**
>
> **Create a Lead Magnet.**
>
> It's time to create your first Lead Magnet using the process we've just outlined above. You can use your piece of content from the previous chapter as a base or start something new. Don't spend more than two hours on the first iteration. If you want to turn it into a big thing later on, great. But start SMALL.
>
> Go to MillionDollarWeekend.com to get Lead Magnet templates! (See what I did there?)

Now that you have an email list that's starting to grow, let's enable it to work for you 24/7.

Set Up Your Cash Register

What's your first action after you read a really great book? You go look for other books by that author. Right? Point is, if people like your stuff, they want more.

At the exact moment your customer is interacting with or just found your business, they are MOST excited about it. So that's when you want to funnel them into other experiences with you instead of letting them go. Because they WANT YOU.

So what does this mean?

This means that instead of waiting for a week or more after they subscribe to send them their first email, you set up an autoresponder and hit them up right away. And better yet, send them your BEST stuff so you know they'll have a great experience when they're dining at the email restaurant of you.

An autoresponder is a tool that automatically sends an email or a sequence of emails to specific groups of people in response to specific behavior—in this case, to your new subscribers when they sign up for your business's newsletter and news at your landing page.

Think of it as a personal assistant who works more or less for free twenty-four hours a day (don't feel bad about it—they don't mind!).

Every email provider has an autoresponder. Again I recommend SendFox.com, but you can use Mailchimp.com or ConvertKit.com as well.

Here's the three-step progression of emails that I've found works best:

1. Welcome Email

SUBJECT: You're awesome

Thanks for joining OkDork. You are awesome!

Over 17 years of working online I've learned some things:

- #30 at Facebook and helped launch mobile, status updates, and more
- #4 at Mint and led growth to 1 million users within 1 year
- Started AppSumo, which is now an $85M/year business

And now, I want to help you on your journey to living the life you want.

What could I write to provide value to you?

Love you,
Noah "tacos" Kagan

---

2. **Connection Email**

SUBJECT: Connect with me on LinkedIn

Howdy amigo,

Send me a connection request on LinkedIn to help share our relationships, see behind-the-scenes thoughts on marketing, startups, and more...

Hugs,
Noah

3. **Content Email**

SUBJECT: Starting an 8-figure business with $50

I started AppSumo in March 2010.

In one weekend, with $50, I launched version 1 of the site. It was simple.

12 years later, Sumo Group has grown into an 8-figure business.

Starting a business can be hard. But I want to show you an easier way:

Here's how I built AppSumo.com for $50.

Enjoy,
Noah

First, the *Welcome Email* is just what it says it is: a big bear hug of a welcome telling your new subscriber how happy you are that they just joined your band of pirates and what sort of stuff they should expect from you.

Remember, this welcome will arrive at the moment they are most willing to participate in your business. That's why every time someone joins my list, I ask one question in my Welcome Email: "What could I write to provide value to you?"

In that way, you'll get tons of content ideas and know exactly what your subscribers want.

A MAJOR thing here is one-by-one marketing. This is personally engaging with each new subscriber. When you're starting out, *every single person matters*. Frankly, everyone in your audience matters forever, but *especially* at the beginning, you should respond to every single new subscriber. I STILL do this for nearly every single email and did for most of my YouTube comments.

Second, with the *Connection Email*, you're explicitly asking them to connect with you on social media, by following you on Instagram, LinkedIn, Facebook, Twitter, and so on.

Finally, the *Content Email* is where you give them a piece of great content—a blog post like Chris Von Wilpert's, a video, or the invite to an event.

If you're an interior designer, this is where you might show them your work and get them excited. Or for Sleep Sumo, Julien could send a blog post about the science of sleeping under or on top of the covers (you know there are two types of sleepers in the world!).

Now, one final tip before we move on.

I always advise sending your best *Content Email* (free course, best articles or videos, content most useful for your audience, etc.) in the beginning.

The reason is simple. For each subscriber, open rates usually start high, then decline after a few emails. So show subscribers your best work to minimize that decline.

> **CHALLENGE**
>
> **Set up an autoresponder.**
>
> I happen to think SendFox.com (I helped build it) is pretty darned good, but there are a bunch of others that I recommend, like ConvertKit.com and Mailchimp.com.
>
> Go to MillionDollarWeekend.com for a free tutorial and templates you can copy for yourself.

The Law of 100

In 2018, I started a podcast called **Noah Kagan Presents**. I did around 50 episodes total and got about 30,000 downloads an episode.

And then I gave it up completely.

Does that sound familiar to you?

Have you been trying to start a business, learn chess, grow your social presence, or maybe play guitar . . . and you also gave up a little bit early?

Compare that to the story of the guys from Buffer.com.

I remember these guys commenting on my blog in 2010, telling me that they were doing social sharing, we're starting this business, blah, blah . . . and I remember thinking to myself, *They are so not going to stick with that idea and fail.*

I don't know why I was such a hater. What I do know is, it's over ten years later now and their business is doing $20 million in recurring revenue.

So what's the difference between my podcast and Buffer?

They stuck with it. And I didn't.

To avoid fails like that, I've come to rely on an effective

framework I call **the Law of 100**. Let me explain using a crazy study from the University of Florida.

Photography professor Jerry Uelsmann split his photography into two groups: the Quantity group and the Quality group.

The Quantity group had to take 100 pictures to get an A grade by the end of the semester, and the Quality group could turn in just one photo by the end of the semester—but it had to be perfect to get the A.

Can you guess what happened?

The Quantity group kicked the Quality group's ass—in terms of quality!

Why?

The Quantity group experimented more! They took tons of photos, learned from their mistakes each time, spent more time in the darkroom, and they got better with time.

That's what the Law of 100 is about.

It's simple: Whatever you put yourself to, do it 100 times before you even THINK of stopping. This stops you from succumbing to what Seth Godin calls "the dip," the moment in a long slog between starting and when mastery sets in where you start hating the work and you want to quit.

For me with my podcast, I wanted to get 100,000 downloads an episode, so when I only got to 30,000 downloads, I was discouraged and gave up completely—after just 50 tries. What's wild is (a) if I was getting 30,000 downloads today, it would be a top podcast; and (b) since I've restarted and committed, I'm at 7,500 downloads an episode. A painful but valuable lesson.

Lean in and commit to 100 reps. (Think of this as doing reps and practicing as opposed to failing or succeeding.) This changes your mindset and makes it much easier to sustain forward motion when things get tough.

The key is to set up a system that helps you get your 100 reps done *without thinking about the results.*

The solution to all the doubt that will inevitably creep up on you is to commit to your first 100—whatever it is for you—with complete disregard for your results.

- If you want to start a YouTube channel, publish 100 videos.
- If you're doing a newsletter, write 100 emails.
- If you're starting a new hobby like chess or guitar, practice for 100 days.
- If you're creating a business, directly pitch 100 customers.

Just focus on that first 100. Don't worry about whether people are watching or liking or engaging or buying or following—just put it out. For the first 100, it's about your doing it, rather than anyone else's liking it.

Once that's done, you can decide whether you want to give it up or not.

The lesson here is to do today what you need in order to reach your end goal. Step by step. Session by session. Video by video and email by email. With each iteration, you keep improving, a little bit.

The Law of 100 is about the power of consistency—the only way to get to greatness.

CHALLENGE

The Law of 100.

Commit to doing 100 emails, posts, or whatever action will move you closer to your goals. To live up to your commitment, use the Law of 100 Grid below to track your progress—and don't break the chain!

TASK: _____

1	2	3	4	5	6	7	8	9	10
11	12	13	14	15	16	17	18	19	20
21	22	23	24	25	26	27	28	29	30
31	32	33	34	35	36	37	38	39	40
41	42	43	44	45	46	47	48	49	50
51	52	53	54	55	56	57	58	59	60
61	62	63	64	65	66	67	68	69	70
71	72	73	74	75	76	77	78	79	80
81	82	83	84	85	86	87	88	89	90
91	92	93	94	95	96	97	98	99	100

Get a digital copy of the Law of 100 tracker at MillionDollarWeekend.com.

CHAPTER 8

The Growth Machine

My Battle-Tested Growth Playbook

"Sorry, Noah, you're not good enough yet to market my company."

That's how Mint.com founder Aaron Patzer said no to me the first time I asked him to be his director of marketing. And it was true: I was no marketer then, and I had no experience or real plan.

But after being fired from Facebook, I was desperate to show the world I wasn't a loser. I came back to him with a detailed marketing plan I'd use again and again, for the next fifteen years. And then I pitched it to Aaron as an offer that can't be refused: "I'll get you 100,000 users in six months before you've even launched the product," I told him. "If I don't hit my target, you don't have to pay me."

I executed the marketing plan with two key components: sponsoring very targeted financial bloggers and writing the best finance content online. Six months later, in September 2007, Mint officially launched with 1 MILLION users. I had exceeded my goal ten times over and got my first six-figure salary!

Since then, I have grown eight different million-dollar businesses with the same marketing plan. Sumo.com reached 1 billion impressions in twelve months. SendFox.com got 10,000 customers in six months and 850,000-plus YouTube subscribers in the past few years.

I've learned how to create a marketing plan to repeatably grow businesses. There are an unlimited number of marketing strategies out there, but there are five questions I keep coming back to for every single business. Here are my five exact questions to create your own marketing plan (and if you want to see the original Mint marketing plan, go to MillionDollarWeekend.com):

1. What is your one goal for this year?
2. Who exactly is your customer and where can you find them?
3. What is one marketing activity you can double down on?
4. How can you delight your first 100 customers?
5. If you HAD to double your business with no money in thirty days, what would you do?

Merely copying the plan and then hoping and praying won't work. That's gambling. That's luck as a strategy.

It's impossible to know which marketing strategies will work for you. Blogging worked for me at Mint.com but has never worked for AppSumo.com. Paid ads work at AppSumo, but we couldn't make the economics work for my OkDork

If you HAD to double your business with no money in thirty days, what would you do?

brand. Ultimately, this is all about setting up a process that helps you identify which tactics work for you.

Before we start marketing, we have to choose a goal to work toward.

1. Set a single hyper-focused exact goal.

Mark Zuckerberg sat me down in his office, and I started pitching how we could sell tickets inside Facebook events.

"Mark, we are not profitable, and we need the money. Let's try this out," I pleaded.

He said *no*.

Then he took a dry-erase marker and wrote on the board: *GROWTH*. And next to it he wrote a number: *1 BILLION*.

And proceeded to explain that every single activity we did should be focused ONLY on growing our user base to 1 billion users.

A laser focus on the outcome and strict prioritizing drove the company to where it is today.

That's the moment it clicked for me, and I use it to this day to choose one very specific goal to work toward.

First off, you need to set a goal. That means choosing a number. For AppSumo in the beginning, the goal was 100,000 email addresses. Everything else (revenue from purchases, sharing deals, visibility, brand awareness) is rooted in that single number. We noticed that if we could grow that number, everything else grew, too. Other examples could be:

- The monthly Freedom Number you chose in chapter 1
- 1,000 YouTube subscribers
- $1 million in net revenue
- Fifty clients

Your goal is the one number that matters most. Starting with the destination makes planning the route much easier.

> **PRO TIP:** Be specific. One of the most common mistakes I see from entrepreneurs when they set goals is they say they want "more." More revenue, more traffic, more downloads. But how much and by when?

Now add a time frame. A terrible goal is "I want to be rich." That's totally meaningless. What's the number? A better one is "I want to be worth $1 million." There's no time frame. And without a time frame, there's no urgency. So what's a goal we can work with?

"I want to be worth $1 million in three years."

Me likey.

Once you have a goal and a time frame, you can break down your goal into a timeline of smaller targets. Besides making your goals feel more achievable, having a timeline is crazy motivating because you get to tick off smaller wins on the way to achieving your overall target.

Recently, my main goal was to grow my YouTube.com/okdork channel to 500,000 subscribers (number) within one year (time frame). So I set out a monthly schedule, keeping in mind that I'd probably want to start slow and then accelerate as I test my different tactics and double down on the ones that work.

Here's how I've modeled my goal of 500,000 subscribers:

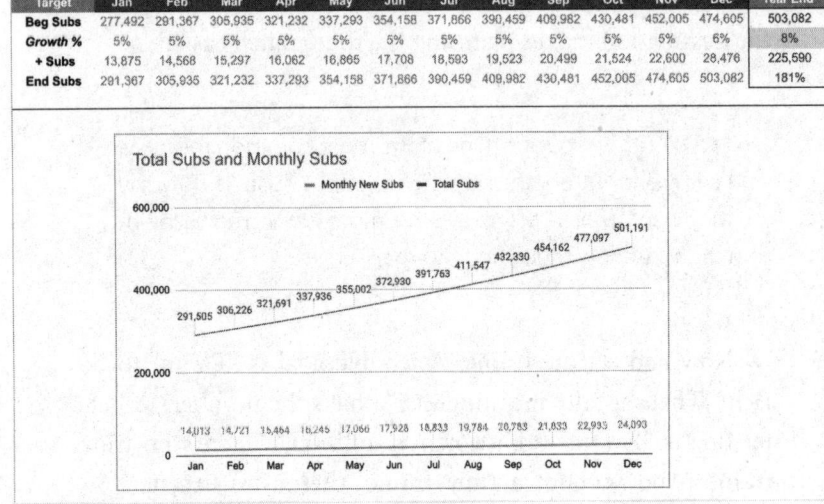

This spreadsheet gives me tangible monthly targets.

- July's goal is 18,833 subscribers.
- August's goal is 19,784 subscribers.
- September's goal is 20,783 subscribers.

Knowing the numbers is an extremely helpful way to stay focused on one objective. I can say no to a lot of ideas that might be fun to try but don't bring results.

You've got a timeline. Great. What's next?

2. Create your Marketing Experiment List.

"I'm tweeting twice a day and it's going to help me sell my new course to Realtors," said one of my students. Let's call him Ricky the Realtor.

"Oh, really?" I responded.

"Yeah, every day I tweet things and then I use a new tool I

bought to reply to people so they can follow me and eventually become my customers," Ricky said.

"Rightttttt," I said, pretty sure this wasn't going to work out.

Fast-forward. Many days later, I asked Ricky how many sales he had made.

$0.

"I say this in a judgment-free way, BUT have you tried any other marketing ideas to help sell to Realtors?"

He had not.

Before you paddle quickly in the wrong direction, we MUST quickly try different marketing experiments to figure out which ones we can double down on.

The best way to do this is by using an Experiment-Based Marketing list to plan and track your marketing strategies.

Let me give you a real-world example: the story of Daniel Bliss.

Daniel is a hobbyist climber, a Canadian, a great guy—and the winner of the AppSumo Make a $1,000 a Month Business getaway to Austin, where we personally worked together for a week on his business.

Our goal for his getaway was to turn his climbing hobby into a real business, making $4,000 a month. Getting to his Freedom Number would allow him to quit his day job as a postal worker and go rock climbing in Thailand. Spoiler alert: He's enjoying a lot of pad thai now.

Daniel was smartly focused on solving one of his own problems. He's a rock climber, and it hurt his neck to lean back and look up while he was belaying (standing on the ground helping the climber above him). He wanted to buy glasses to let him look up without craning his neck.

He had already found a manufacturer on Alibaba to make the glasses he wanted, with mirrors that let you see up while looking forward. Daniel had also already validated his business by getting a few pairs made and selling twelve pairs by hand. He sold two pairs to a couple he met while climbing and the rest to his climbing group.

But now he was stuck. How do you grow beyond that? Like most entrepreneurs, Daniel did the obvious yet wrong things. He wasted time tricking out his Shopify website with bells and whistles. He investigated intellectual property laws to protect his design. He stalked competitors.

Let's fix that...

First, we worked backwards from his goal to determine how many he wanted to sell to get to $4,000 a month. Goal.

$4,000 profit a month

The glasses sell for $60 a pair with shipping

He makes $24 per pair sold

$4,000/$24 = 166 glasses sold each month

Basically, 5 to 6 pairs of glasses a day

I can't stress how important this is, so I'll repeat it again: WORK BACKWARDS FROM YOUR GOAL!

Next, we created a list of marketing strategies that could get Daniel to his goal:

Source	Expected Sales	Actual Sales
Personal network + referrals	30	???
Sale to Vancouver Rock Climbing Group	20	???
Wholesale	50	???

Source	Expected Sales	Actual Sales
Marketplaces: eBay	25	???
Giveaways	25	???
Facebook ads	16	???
Total	166 (his goal)	

Now, Daniel had only one hour a week to do this, **so I asked him, "If you could use only two of the marketing activities, what would they be?"** They were also the marketing experiments with highest expected sales.

He chose:

1. Personal network + referrals
2. Wholesale selling to climbing gyms/online stores

Starting with his top two channels, Daniel first searched Facebook for every single friend who listed climbing in their profiles and added them to a sheet. You can also do this just by looking at contacts on your phone. Then he individually messaged them.

Hey <first name>

Hope you've been awesome.

I saw you like climbing. Me, too!

My neck always hurts when I belay, so I created super affordable belay goggles.

Have about 10 available. Are you interested?

Climb on,
Daniel

A few sales came just from messaging his Facebook friends. SCORE.

Then we created a list of every rock-climbing store offline and online in Canada.

1. Search Google for "rock climbing Vancouver" or search "rock climbing" on Yelp.
2A. Go to websites listed and get the owner's name (if possible), email, and phone number.
   OR
2B. Hire someone on Fiverr.com or Craigslist to go through every listing and add them on a sheet.

And we messaged them, too.

SUBJECT: Helping you make an extra $1,000 at your climbing gym

Hey Colleen,

Hope things have been amazing with you.

I've been working with climbing gyms like yours and wanted to hook up your members with my new belay glasses.

www.belayshades.com (people go nuts over them)

Was thinking, we can email your members with a special discount just for you and we split the profit evenly.

Be a great way for you to make a profit and hook up your members at the same time.

Can you let me know by this Friday if this sounds appealing to you?

Rock on,
Dan Bliss

Afterwards, Daniel had time and tried several other marketing strategies listed:

We posted on marketplaces. This involves posting your product to sites that already have your customers like eBay, Etsy, Craigslist, or Amazon. All totally free, too.

And after waiting a few days—no sales.

We tried Facebook and Google advertising. Here's the exact Facebook ad we created:

This drove 0 sales.

We also did giveaways. Daniel reached out to various Facebook pages and Meetup groups and bloggers related to climbing and offered to send them a sample and then, if they liked the glasses, to grant them a special price to sell to their members.

SUBJECT: Free belay Glasses for you and your <group name>
Hey <Club Leader>

Your group looks awesome! Glad to see the climbing community growing in <location>.

Wanted to let you know about these cool new belay glasses for rock climbers, called Belay Shades.

Would love to send you a free pair to try out. If you like them, I'll happily give your group a special price you can share with your members.

Just email me by <two days from when email is sent> with an address we can ship to, and we will send you a pair.

Belay On!
Daniel

This did not produce ANY results.

But then . . . Daniel got an email from a large online site he'd contacted named Sierra Trading saying they were interested in the glasses.

HOLY CRAP! He'd been waiting weeks to hear back from small local stores. Now an online provider was finally responding within a day.

The order placed was for $4,200!

After thirty days, here's Daniel's final result:

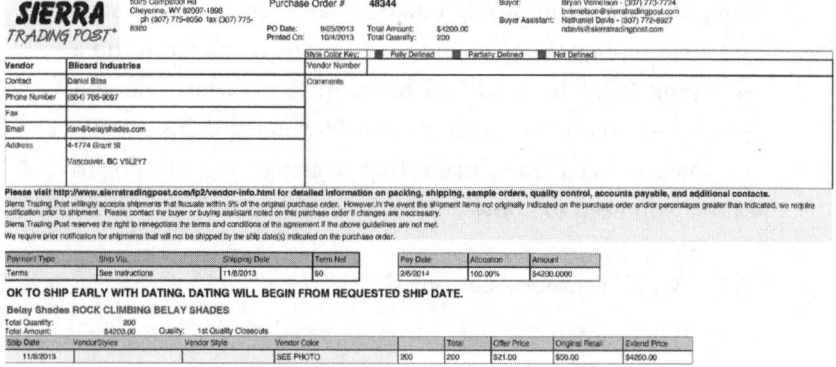

Daniel's actual sale of $4,200

Source	Expected Sales	Actual Sales
Reach out to friends + referrals	30	9
Sale to Vancouver Rock Climbing Group	20	11
Wholesale options	50	217
Marketplaces—eBay	25	0
Giveaways	25	0
Facebook ads	16	0
Total	166 (his goal)	237

The point here is, you never know what's going to work when it comes to marketing. To find the thing that does work, what you need is a process of small experiments—based on your BEST GUESS of what might work. It's all about prioritizing tactics and ruthlessly testing them!

Daniel tried six different experiments in thirty days. He

thought wholesaling would make 50 sales. Turns out it made 200+. He thought eBay would do 30 units; turns out it did a whopping 0. So he modified his plan to go wholesale and doubled down on that, since it made 90 percent of his sales.

Now let's get a list of marketing strategies you can do. To do that you need to know:

1. Who is your ideal customer?
2. Where are they?

Who is your ideal customer?

- At Mint, we focused on personal finance bloggers and tech professionals.
- At AppSumo, our customer is Marketing Agency Matt, who is a solopreneur.
- At OkDork, my customer is an underdog looking for inspiration on their business journey.

The best way I found to figure out your ideal customer is to look for patterns with your existing ones:

> Think about what's in common with your existing customers. Certain age? Common interest? Specific gender? Certain hobbies? From a specific area?

> **CHALLENGE**
>
> **Who's your customer?**
>
> Describe to me who your ideal customer is.
>
> The MORE specific the better. Think about their gender, age, location, and anything else that makes them unique.
>
> _____
> _____
> _____

Next, where can you find more of these ideal customers?

Look where you found your previous ones and ask your existing customers!

Here's the exact message I still send to people to this day:

> Hey Maria,
>
> Thank you so much for being a customer.
>
> Where's the one specific place you'd expect to learn about my product?

Now make a list of these places where we can find more of these people.

For example, with Daniel:

Who: People who rock climb outdoors at least once a week.

Where: North America/Canada, belong to a rock-climbing gym, purchase things from sporting goods stores, read *Outside* magazine, are fans of Alex Honnold (the free soloist climber), are in meetups/online groups to talk about climbers, watch specific YouTubers who teach new climbing techniques, and eat energy food like CLIF Bars.

If you can't think of where, here's a list of generic marketing ideas to get you going:

- **Contacting your network:** The number one place you should look for customers is in your own existing network. The benefit is that people already know you, so making the sale is easier.
- **Paid ads:** Reach out to potential customers on search engines like Bing and Google, so your name will appear when certain keywords are searched.
- **Social ads:** Target your audience through ads on social channels like Twitter and Facebook, Reddit, TikTok, or LinkedIn.
- **Content marketing:** Create and publish content (blogs, podcasts, videos) with the goal of generating interest in your product/service.
- **Cold outreach:** Speak directly to potential customers. This could mean picking up the phone and calling potential customers or sending cold emails to prospects.
- **Target market blogs:** Sponsor posts and content on popular blogs within your target market.
- **Influencer marketing:** Identify and build relationships with individuals who have influence over your target market (for example, high-profile bloggers or Instagrammers).
- **PR:** Pitch the press and bloggers in your niche to cover your story.
- **SEO:** Search engine optimization is another reliable way to grow your traffic, but it takes time. Do some keyword research on sites like AnswerThePublic or SpyFu to discover what people in your niche are talking about. Create hyper-targeted content to drive traffic.

- **Giveaways:** Round up some epic prizes, create a sweepstakes page... and promote the shit out of it.
- **Collaborations:** Appear on other podcasts/shows/newsletters/YouTube channels.

After you figured out your marketing ideas lists, we need to estimate expected sales from these ideas.

Setting your expected sales is one of the most important parts of your strategy. These targets will give you something to measure against and help you identify where you can double down in the future.

So how do you go about setting targets for your sources?

The most important aspect of this process is not to worry about being exact. It's to make decent guesses so you can have a framework to prioritize and double down on your sources.

When setting your targets, the trick is to use your BEST GUESS; it doesn't have to be a super-accurate number. It's all to help you PRIORITIZE your marketing activities. Over time, you'll get better at this.

Here's an example for thirty days of sales:

Marketing Experiments	Expected Sales
1. SEO: Write four blog posts	10
2. Contact everyone in my network	25
3. Call my aunt Rhonda	1
4. Post in Meetup group	5
5. Post flyer	9
Total	40

This spreadsheet helps you prioritize your time by focusing on the largest expected sales items first.

Another option is to add a column for Time: how long it will take you to do the different activities. You can use this to see which activities will not take much time but still get sales.

Also, you can consider including cost if you're doing ads, but I encourage people to not spend money on marketing at first. Exhaust your free options.

> **CHALLENGE**
>
> **Where are your customers?**
>
> Now list at least five places your customers are and how many sales in thirty days you think you can get from them.

Marketing Experiments	Expected Sales
1.	
2.	
3.	
4.	
5.	
Total	

3. Double down on what works.

There's a golden rule to marketing tactics I want you to repeat after me:

Find what works and double down on it; find what doesn't work and kill it.

Even now, I can forget this golden rule. At Sumo.com a little while ago, we started massively promoting our Instagram posts to convert our followers into customers when we saw that (1) we had more than 100,000 Instagram followers and our posts were getting a lot of likes, and (2) Instagram is cool and works for tons of other people.

And you know what? It literally drove zero dollars—$0!—but it took us six months and $20,000 spent before we admitted it wasn't working and killed it.

The simple lesson here is that you need to find the tactics that are right for your business—not just what's the "hottest" marketing strategy this month.

Now, there's nothing wrong with experimenting and trying new channels—but you need to set time limits to stop if something isn't working. I find thirty days is more than enough to get results from your marketing experiments.

That's why for an entrepreneur it's important to have a lazy mindset. If something's too hard and not working after a good try? Give up and move on!

Double down on the experiments that work the best.

Kill the experiments that don't meet expectations.

The point is to continue only if you see traction. Seriously, be ruthless. Even $100 a day or thirty minutes a day is an opportunity cost of time and money that could be spent elsewhere. For instance, when I wanted to grow my online presence in 2019, I tried everything: Twitter, TikTok, blogging, Instagram, YouTube . . . I know. I know. Sounds familiar, right?

After thirty days of trying all of them, I forced myself to choose between them. By then it had become clear in terms of the amount of audience I was getting relative to the work it took that one was vastly better than the rest: I stopped doing every other channel and went all in on YouTube.

I like to check back against my assumptions weekly (and sometimes daily) to measure my marketing plan progress.

The first couple of weeks of your strategy will likely feature a lot of experimentation and testing until you find what works and what doesn't. Generally, you'll need a month to see if a channel is promising or not.

Once you find a channel or tactic that works, do more of it until it stops working. For someone like Daniel (the climbing glasses guy), that means focusing his efforts on online wholesalers, which were his number one sales channel by far.

Take the tactic that works and double it. Remember, the lazy mindset works!

> ### CHALLENGE
>
> **What marketing strategies can I double down on?**
>
> Let's update your original marketing experiments sheet with actual sales. This should make it obvious which experiments to double down on and which ones to kill.

Fill this out right now:

Marketing Experiments	Expected Sales	Actual Sales
1.		
2.		
3.		
4.		
5.		
Total		

BUT instead of focusing ONLY on your new customers, let's take advantage of the ones you already have.

4. Make Your First 100 Customers Happier

How would you double your business if you COULD NOT get any new customers?

This will help you think of ways you can overdeliver to your current customers. Because the biggest growth lever in business is customer retention and referrals. If you're just starting out, every referral can literally double your business.

Here are some examples of how I've done this:

When I started growing my YouTube channel, I personally replied to every YouTube comment. This made the audience feel special and connected to me.

With Gambit, I gave my personal phone number to every customer even when we were making $20-million-plus a year. That level of customer service and attention to detail is how we were able to grow so fast.

In the first years of AppSumo.com—and even today—I personally write to customers to see what they like and dislike about us. They invariably start their reply by saying, "You're Noah and you're writing to me? Really?" But by the end they're thrilled—and they're telling their friends.

Here's an email from one of the first ever AppSumo customers:

> On 17 May 2010 13:08, Noah <noah@appsumo.com> wrote:
>
> > Hey Will
>
> Thank you so much for buying! We are going to enable your Pro account today and email you (:
>
> I wanted to ask you a few questions if you have two minutes:
>
> -What made you interested in buying Imgur?
>
> -What other websites/services would you want big discounts on?

-Any suggestions or things you would have wanted to see on our website, appsumo.com?

Feel free to spread the word: http://appsumo.com/

Your Friend,
Noah

Will Derrick <email removed>
to me ▼

Hi Noah,

I do love Reddit and Imgur is the best image hosting for Reddit. I like the service and want to support it, having this offer on Reddit seems like a brilliant way of supporting all involved. :) It's like an awesome Reddit discount.

It would be good to mention clearly that it's not instant, I didn't realize when I ran through the process I wouldn't just be presented with a code once the PayPal had been processed. Waiting isn't a problem, but "Buy now" is a little misleading when it's "Pay now, we'll send you your upgrade within 24 hours." Nowadays I expect everything to be instant, it's weird when it takes time.

I'd love a discount on my Napster subscription, Battlefunds on Battlefield: Heroes or my Spotify subscription. I've just signed up to the beta of Flattr, but I can't see how a discount would work with those guys!

Cheers,
Will

This is not scalable. That's the point.

The other key is to keep overdelivering and make your current customers as happy as possible. The benefits of this are twofold:

- Happy customers will refer your business to their friends.
- Happy customers are more likely to spend more cash and buy your new products or services.

The longer you retain customers, the more opportunity you have to earn more revenue from them.

As well, every step of the way you can get feedback to make your product or service even better. Ask your customers this: "What is one thing we can do today that will make you twice as happy with us?"

A great example to leave you with is Nick Bare from Bare Performance Nutrition.

Noah Kagan
@noahkagan

When Nick Bare was growing BPN Supplements from $1K - $100K per month, he wrote every US customer a hand-written thank you note.

While he was in KOREA.

Best way to grow your business:

Make your customers feel special.

6:04 PM · Sep 2, 2022 · Hypefury

2 Retweets   56 Likes

This is a guy who was deployed overseas in Korea, had to get up at four a.m. to do his side hustle, and made it a point to personally message every one of his customers. This was the foundation that helped him build his supplement business into a seven-figure company today!

CHALLENGE
Make your customers happy.

Ask one customer: "What is one thing I can do today that will make you twice as happy with us?"

TLDR of Growth

In your MDW journal, answer these five questions:

1. What is your one goal for this year?

2. Who exactly is your customer and where can you find them?

3. What is one marketing activity you can double down on?

4. How can you delight your first 100 customers?

5. If you HAD to double your business with no money in thirty days, what would you do?

CHAPTER 9

52 Chances This Year

Using Systems and Routines to Design the Business, and Life, You Want

In 2014, AppSumo was doing about $4 million a year in revenue, and I was taking home about $150,000 of it. I could finally afford everything I've dreamed of having.

I made it!

And I felt like shit.

It wasn't exhaustion. That's something else—something temporary and physical. This was deeper. The reality was, I felt lost and sad—with a misery that had set deep roots in my soul—and it was tainting everything else in my life. I didn't love a lot of the products we were selling. I didn't love a lot of the people at my company. I didn't love where I was living. I didn't love my girlfriend.

It made zero sense. How could I be this successful—or "successful"—but feel this unhappy?

I started trying a lot of things to cure the dread I felt every morning as my eyes opened: books, Reddit forums, therapy, intermittent fasting, cold showers (my reaction: This just sucks. Now I'm sad *and* freezing).

It all came to a head a month later, at an affiliate marketing conference when I was talking to my friend Rob and I told him how sad I was and how soul-numbing my "successful" routine felt. "It's sucking me dry," I said. "I feel empty."

I'll never forget crying in a meeting. I sat in on a presentation in a windowless conference room as some dude droned on about scaling ad campaigns, and my eyes welled up with tears. I felt a hollowness that scared me. Wasn't success supposed to make my life better?

Something had to change.

And that's when I decided to go on a spiritual quest. Just like the Beatles and Steve Jobs did when they were seeking enlightenment. It seemed to help them, and I prayed it would do the same for me! It was so clear now: I had to *leave* my life to find myself.

That settled it. I'd travel to India, just like the Beatles and Steve.

I traveled to Rishikesh in northern India and spent time at the ashram of the Maharishi Mahesh Yogi—the same guru who developed Transcendental Meditation and taught it to the Beatles. I spent time in a cave with a sadhu who'd left the whole world behind. I hung out with yogis in Goa hoping it would spark something. I walked around most of India looking to escape my comfort zone, willing to risk everything for a life change in my quest for a self-discovery experience.

And after a month it dawned on me . . .

After actually growing a multimillion-dollar business, I was doing what I thought I should be doing versus what I really wanted.

I was told I had to promote one product a day to hyper-

Picture of me in India—rough, I know

scale the business. So we were pushing out products like a $49 PDF showing how to make iPhone apps that wasn't useful. I was told by my $10,000 a day business coach to aggressively hire more people to get even more profits. So we went from four people to twenty people in six months. I was told to act more professional. So we reduced the quirky branding on the AppSumo website. I was told to be in meetings and conduct formal performance reviews. So my calendar was full of meetings with employees and partners I didn't care for.

I became an entrepreneur to live the life I wanted, not to do what the stereotypical CEO should do. And being an entrepreneur, I had the power to make changes.

Starting a business all comes back to freedom. That does not mean everything you do is to always maximize profits. Maybe freedom means spending time with your kids in the morning and relaxing in the afternoon. Or working remotely while practicing your tango lessons in Argentina. Or making a product just 'cause you think it's cool.

On my flight home I decided to promote only products I could 100 percent stand behind on AppSumo. I committed to removing friends and colleagues who were toxic regardless of their "rockstar-ness." I wanted to keep our product ratings systems via tacos, not stars, as everyone else does. I arranged my day so I had no meetings before noon and spent Fridays drinking happy hour (all day) with great friends like Neville. These might seem like small changes, but these are the reasons I became an entrepreneur. To live my life, my way.

My turnaround wasn't immediate. I still have to work on all of these things today. But entrepreneurship and *Million Dollar Weekend* has taught me more about myself than everything else combined. I've learned this: **the first step to getting all you want in the world is allowing yourself to want it—and facing the fears necessary to be able to get what you want**.

Some people work a steady job for $70,000 a year and are extremely happy. You accomplished your dream. Yay. But many of us have other dreams. There's no wrong dream. *Million Dollar Weekend* is for those who have a dream to build something themselves.

Remember Daniel Bliss, the postal worker who created belay shades? Here's his advice for you:

> The Million Dollar Weekend process was instrumental in sparking my entrepreneurial spirit. My initial business idea gradually evolved, and within a couple of years, I became the main distributor for a European climbing brand in America. Over the course of the next decade, I closed the business, having achieved something approaching a million in sales.

The earnings from the business didn't just sit in a bank account. I was able to invest and create wealth, which has opened up so many opportunities. It's allowed me to pursue personal passions, like traveling and training as a freediving instructor in Egypt, and fund my ongoing education in computer science and programming.

What's more, I've managed to strike a balance that has significantly improved my quality of life. I still work part-time at the post office and dabble in side hustles, but my main focus has always been to increase my freedom, continue my learning journey, and make the most of the "time freedom" that entrepreneurship has granted me.

Looking ahead, my future is a blank canvas, and while I'm not sure what I'll do next, I know it'll be more interesting than delivering mail eight hours a day!

Looking back, I can honestly say that I am a completely different person because of *Million Dollar Weekend*!

Daniel Bliss out rock climbing—living his million dollar life

> **CHALLENGE**
>
> **Let's share your story of success to help others.**
>
> Just as you learned from Daniel, your words can inspire someone else.
>
> Send an email to noah@MillionDollarWeekend.com or post on social media and tag me @noahkagan with how you've improved your life. I'll share it on MillionDollarWeekend.com. The fact you're reading and taking action is leading you in the right direction.

In this final chapter, we are going to determine the dreams you want to fulfill and prioritize the important tasks to achieve those dreams. Then we'll explore building a supportive network who can keep you accountable and help you accomplish so much more.

Bringing Out Your Dreams

In a j-o-b, you must accept the system you are in. As an entrepreneur, you get to design your own system.

The challenge of your business—and your life—is designing a system that optimizes for your overall happiness.

We all get into entrepreneurship to fulfill our goals of personal freedom and joy. But your version of success is unique from that of every other entrepreneur's, which means you get to design your own path.

In order to do this, you have to believe that you *can* redesign your life to create space for the fun and fulfillment that you deserve. Permission granted.

Do not let fear hold you back. Designing the life of your dreams is where you truly become rich. So keep moving!

Entrepreneurship is your chance to build your work around your life, not be swallowed up by it. The problem is, as an entrepreneur and maybe a spouse or parent as well, you have a ton of stuff pulling at you from moment to moment. That constant chaos keeps you from consistently winning your days. It is one of the greatest impediments to achieving fun and fulfillment. When you can't focus, you lose control.

So how do we prevent ourselves from losing focus on our goals, or losing control of our lives?

Let's design a checklist to regain your focus and I'll show you mine.

Dream Year Checklist

Imagine your best year ever. Close your eyes. Picture eating Chipotle with all the guacamole you want, you're making your Freedom Number, you spend half your day researching plants 'cause you love it, and you get to live in multiple places. Your dreams can become reality only if you think about what you really want.

Here's an excerpt from my recent Dream Year:

- ❏ AppSumo is THE marketplace for software and easily grows to $30 million.
- ❏ We find a dream house: pool, garage, NICE kitchen with great house for entertaining that is ALSO reasonably priced.
- ❏ Amazing experience in Spain with Ian and lots of drinking + biking.

- ☐ Grow YouTube channel to 500,000 subscribers.
- ☐ Get an airplane pilot's license.
- ☐ My health gets into the best condition ever from biking.
- ☐ Continue biking across America.
- ☐ I hang out with Joe Rogan on his podcast talking about something unique I did.
- ☐ I create a business Netflix show that goes super-popular.
- ☐ I write a popular book that's not another biz or self-help book that people really resonate with.
- ☐ Do one week of solo travel.
- ☐ Visit a mountain biking city—Asheville, Sun Valley, Jackson Hole, Sedona.
- ☐ Fly my parents to spend time with me in Europe.
- ☐ I do an RV/camper trip to the Grand Canyon, including biking along the way, maybe some disc golf, fires, diners, breweries (maybe with my brother?).

You're going to start by writing down how you'd love this year to turn out for you. This Dream Year isn't just "I'm gonna have a nice house and my business will rock it." Include the specifics—where you're living, what you're doing, how you feel, where you travel to, etc.

This is to inspire you about all the things you can do in your life. Then really dial in the ones that feel important to you. I've found it also helps me dream bigger: "Hot damn, I can do all these inspiring things!"

Remember: This is a DREAM YEAR. That means dreaming big and not worrying about the how. All you're doing right now is creating a vision for the year that fills you with excitement. Once you have a clear picture of your Dream Year, then you can focus on making it come true.

Instead of being reactive throughout the year and getting thrown off course, you have a chance to focus on what would be an incredible year for YOU and to write it all down.

CHALLENGE

Write out your Dream Year.

Make the checklist detailed and specific.

_____
_____
_____
_____
_____
_____
_____
_____
_____

Turn Your Dream Year into Goals

Now that you have created your Dream Year, it's time to take your dreams and choose and organize them into your goals. This is your life, so PICK the things from your dream list you're MOST excited about. Another key thing is consistency—it's a GOOD thing if you're continuing goals from previous years. Also, I prefer to have fewer things to accomplish but I'm very excited to do them.

Categorize them into four sections: Work, Health, Personal, and Travel.

But feel free to change or add to these however you'd like, it's YOUR life!

Here are the ones I picked from the above year:

Work:
- $30 million for AppSumo
- 500,000 YouTube subscribers
- Finish *Million Dollar Weekend* book

Health:
- Bike across America
- 75,000 push-ups

Personal:
- Complete pilot's license and fly to Albuquerque
- Either donate all the money you make or spend it on yourself and friends
- Get a nice house in Austin

Travel:
- Do one week of solo travel
- Visit a mountain biking city (Asheville, Sun Valley, Jackson Hole, Sedona)
- Trip with parents and brother

Key things about your goals:
- Don't worry about doing everything in your dream year. Really think about which ones would excite you. My rule

of thumb is if you're hesitating on the dream, then it shouldn't make your goals list.
- I don't always accomplish everything on my lists every year. And that's okay. This list is to help you prioritize your time, which we'll talk about next. You can schedule and make sure you are working toward the things you really want to do.
- Over the past ten years I've tried to set super-aggressive goals, but I've found that it's better to aim for more sustainable goals. It's more impressive to find and stick with something than burn out after being impressive for one year.
- This list works for you, not the other way around. If midyear you realize something doesn't matter, change it. I aim to review and update this list only twice a year.

The best way to make sure you accomplish your goals is to see them often. Here's where I put mine.

- On the lock screen of my phone
- On a sticky on my computer
- On a text file that I look at each week
- On the mirror of my bathroom
- On a daily note that I read every day

CHALLENGE

Find one person to send your yearly goals to.

This can be someone who invested $1 in you early on, a friend . . . anyone you trust to check in with you regularly and challenge you on your BS as they help you follow through on your promises.

CHALLENGE
Yearly goals list.

Use the four categories to flush out your yearly goals.

Work
_____
_____
_____

Health
_____
_____
_____

Personal
_____
_____
_____

Travel
_____
_____
_____

Show me YOUR calendar and I'll tell you what's most important to you.

Now that you have your goals, let's help you prioritize your time to avoid the distractions of life.

Coloring Your Calendar

If you fail to plan, you are planning to fail.
—Benjamin Franklin

One hundred and sixty-eight.

We all have the same number of hours in a week, 168. How is it that some people get so much more done than others?

With all the obligations like kids, community, day jobs, hobbies, and more in our lives, you must make sure to allocate time to things that matter.

Show me YOUR calendar and I'll tell you what's most important to you.

Since we've created your goals, we now take those items and place them in your calendar every week.

Here's my calendaring system:

- Put everything in a **Category.**
- Assign a **Color Code** to your categories.
- **Schedule with color** your key weekly priorities.
- Perform a weekly **Sunday accountability (p)review.**

I'm not telling you *how* to spend your time—instead, I'm giving you the systems to make sure you're allocating time toward your goals.

Category and Color Code

Here's a pretty typical screenshot of my calendar showing my weekly schedule:

See a recent version of my calendar at MillionDollarWeekend.com.

Notice something? It's in black and white, since my publisher said color is too expensive, ha!

But everything is color coded!

- Blue = Work
- Green = Health
- Purple = Personal
- Yellow = Travel

What color coding does is help me look at my calendar and instantly see: Am I spending my biggest blocks of time toward my goals? One glance gives me an immediate snapshot of the alignment of my work and priorities—and the mix of each day.

This may stress you out or feel like extra work to do this system. Great, throw it away. I don't care how YOU organize your time. I care that you prioritize your time to work on the goals you have in your life.

This gives me the opportunity to look at my calendar and say, "My stated priority is to build my YouTube audience to 500,000, so why is there so little blue?" and allocate more to it.

> **PRO TIP:** Front-load your priorities, meaning if your main goal is YouTube, focus on it earlier in the week to make sure you're getting done what matters most. I get tired as the week goes on, so I put my most important tasks on Monday and Tuesday.

How to Prioritize the Important Tasks So You Can Accomplish Your Goals

I asked Neville what he did all day and he said he watched *The Simpsons* and played guitar.

Flabbergasted, HUH.

You just sat around your house and did nothing all day??

The guilt and anxiety that would have created in me is astronomical.

The reality of the situation is, Neville prioritizes his week accordingly, sets up systems to make sure the right things get done in his business, and lives his life the way he wants, not others.

Here are the questions I use to prioritize my time:

1. How do I pick what to actually do each week?

Every Sunday, I spend fifteen minutes looking over the past week and setting my tasks for the next one. This is your chance to revisit your yearly goals and choose activities each week to move you closer toward your goals.

2. How do I know if these tasks are moving me in the right direction of my goal?

During my Sunday review I also take my previous Sunday's goals and see how I did against them. This is my chance to evaluate if it moved the needle toward my yearly goal.

It's not to judge or shame yourself, but to keep yourself accountable and continually improve.

3. What if I want to be lazy, do I need to schedule it?

WWND: What Would Neville Do? Hell no. There are days just like Neville's when you want to do nothing. Enjoy it. Use your laziness to your advantage. Are there parts of your work you can outsource, stop doing, or find software to do for you (maybe at a great price on AppSumo.com!)?

4. How can I double down on activities that move me toward my goals?

Whichever activities you love or help you with your goals, put those on repeat. My motto: The more things that are on repeat, the better. If every Monday and Thursday you do three hours of YouTube work starting at one p.m., it becomes habitual. And every Tuesday night I go biking; it's automatic. If the important tasks are automatically added, you free up your brain to focus on the more complex issues that give you energy and move you toward your goals.

With your goals set up, the final piece of living your dream is your support system to help you with accountability and help you succeed. Let's get that set up.

Never Entrepreneur Alone

Ninety percent of my net worth comes from meeting people. When I started AppSumo, I called Andrew Warner, who introduced me to Chad, who became my business partner, CTO, and one of my best friends.

Andrew Chen, whom I met at a startup picnic, changed our business from software bundles to individual deals. That shift increased our company revenue four times that year!

Tim Ferriss (before he was uber famous) tweeted a post that helped drive the second deal I ever did—and he helped drive a shit-ton of sales.

Eric Ries, the lean startup guy, helped me do a SXSW bundle that took AppSumo from six to seven figures.

Neville Medhora helped turn AppSumo emails from ~$100 per send into $10,000 with one email.

Great entrepreneurs have great entrepreneurial communities. There's no such thing as *self-made*. Everyone is team-made.

You're going to get frustrated and lonely as an entrepreneur. That comes with the title, so you've GOT TO HAVE the right group around you—other entrepreneurs who get the unique path you're walking. Especially starting out solo, you need to create your own social infrastructure for support, partnership, learning, and accountability.

Let me show three ways to meet the right people to help you on your business journey.

1. Get an Accountability Buddy

We make better choices and work harder when someone else is observing our behavior. Researchers call it the Hawthorne effect. I call it my number one productivity hack.

There's just something about a little external pressure that helps to keep us honest and on the right track. That's why every Sunday for the past ten years I've sent my friend Adam Gilbert my **Sunday (P)review** email outlining everything I said I'd do last week, how much of it I accomplished, and everything I want to do in the week ahead.

Here's one week's review:

On Sun, Oct 2, at 8:50 PM noah kagan <noah@gmail.com> wrote:

Work:
AppSumo:
- Write up marketing customer journey
  - made great progress on this
- Continue working on Black Friday marketing
  - really dialed in. stoked on this
- Check in with key people at the company one by one
  - did most. finishing up tmrw
- Support finding CFO, VP marketing advisor, and potentially sales advisor
  - marketing advisor moved forward, cfo this week and sales advisor in a week
- Meet with agent to work on book layout/design
  - done. talking more w them.
- Meet with Tahl Raz
  - done
- Review comments from beta readers (ahem, Adam)
  - got great feedback. need more.

Health:
Boxing
Squash
1 epic ride
- done above. no squash. yom kippur

Personal:
Books to read.
- Thinking in systems (physical)
- 4000 weeks (digital)
- The fish that ate the whale (audio)

Go to ACL with Dan
- maybe. tbd. tonight

Travel:
Research cities for parents' Europe trip
- done

Adam replied to this email with: "Nice work on Black Friday, can't wait to see how that turns out. How much time are you spending on your push-ups? I don't see them listed and you said it was an important goal for you this year."

Find someone you respect, probably a peer working toward similar goals, and establish this Sunday ritual to help each other on your journeys. Your buddy is there to support you and celebrate the small victories. This person must reply and hold you accountable. If they never reply or don't call you out when you don't follow through, you need to find a better person.

Accountability buddies? That seems like a potential million-dollar business. Maybe one of you can validate and create it. (:

> **CHALLENGE**
>
> **Accountability buddy.**
>
> **My accountability buddy is:**
> _____
>
> Find one person to send your weekly goals to. For the past ten years, I've worked with Adam Gilbert from mybodytutor.com every week on my yearly goals. Accountability is a superpower.

Go to MillionDollarWeekend.com and join our newsletter. I'll try to connect you with an accountability buddy.

You found an accountability buddy, but how can you meet others to help you succeed at business? Here are two ways that work!

2. Target Prefluencers

I always make an effort to connect with ambitious people BEFORE they make it. It's so much easier to connect with them, help each other, and build actual relationships.

I met Tim in 2007, before he was famous and was trying to promote this book that wasn't out yet called *The 4-Hour Workweek*. I met Ramit Sethi while he was still in college and had just started this blog iwillteachyoutoberich.com, which was making $0. And since then we've all become good friends—and they helped me in everything I've achieved. Remember, it's not about where they are today as much as where you think they are going: I still reach out to ambitious people all the time. A few years ago, I contacted Harry Dry from Marketing Examples, a young kid from England. I loved what he was doing with his newsletter, offering great marketing case studies and copywriting tips. I love connecting with interesting people like him, and this relationship creates a great opportunity to help each other now and in the future. Connect with no expectations.

Today, Harry has 100,000 subscribers on his email list, 30,000 LinkedIn followers, and 140,000 on Twitter. He's doing epic! And we're friends! It would have been harder to connect now, but I got him as a Prefluencer, so it was simple. Just like with Ramit Sethi and Tim Ferriss.

Here are three principles to help you find Prefluencers:

1. Who's doing work you're impressed by?
2. AND who doesn't have a ton of attention and is likely to reply?
3. AND what can you do to help this person?

CHALLENGE

Connect with a Prefluencer.

The easiest way to connect with anyone is to compliment them first WITHOUT asking for anything in return.

The Prefluencer I'm reaching out to:

_____

Send this message:

Hey [first name],

LOVING what you're putting out. [Insert specifically what you liked or how it impacted your life]

Keep going!

[Your Name]

> From here, the person will likely respond and you can open up a dialogue to talk about working together or helping each other in the future. Spam is sending a message asking for something, whereas connecting and building relationships like the above script is just sending a compliment without any expectations.

3. Build Your VIP Network with Referrals

Andrew Chen is one of the most well-known executives in Silicon Valley, a VC partner at Andreessen Horowitz, which specializes in games, AR/VR, metaverse, and other cool stuff.

But back in 2007, I was the only person Andrew knew when he moved to the Bay Area as a twenty-three-year-old.

When he arrived, Andrew knew he needed to widen his network to achieve his dreams and be successful. As an ambitious twenty-something, Andrew wanted to find people ten times better than him.

To build his network, Andrew set a goal: *"Meet five new people per day for my first six months in the Bay Area."*

In less than a year, Andrew was associated with high-profile people like venture capitalist Marc Andreessen (co-founder of Netscape) and entrepreneur Eric Yuan (founder of Zoom). And through that strategy he became a general partner at Andreessen Horowitz, one of the most respected venture capital firms in the world.

His strategy amounted to persistently reaching out, following up, and asking for referrals.

After meeting someone new, Andrew would send them a thank-you email. In it, he would include:

- Highlights from the chat he found interesting
- Follow-ups and to-dos
- Request to meet more people

Wanna try the same in your city? Use the below template next time you meet someone new:

Hi Noah,

Quick thanks for meeting with me. You = awesome.

Here are 3 epic lessons I took away from our chat:

- Look into haptics—great opportunity for biz growth (you mentioned it as the next billion-dollar industry . . . damn!)
- "To be successful, you need to start with things that DON'T scale" ← Great quote you mentioned
- Companies to watch for are Mutual Mobile, Onnit, and Backlinko

Super grateful.

I'm curious: Are there 1–2 other people you believe I should meet?

Thanks again,
Andrew

When he got a new list of people to meet, Andrew would send an intro email with three key points:

- Short blurb about himself
- Value he could provide (that is to say, what's in it for them?)
- Why he was excited to meet them

He'd send this to everyone he was introduced to—personalizing to the entrepreneur or VIP he wanted to meet. And you can do the same.

Telling someone why you are interesting, how you can help, and why you want to meet works like gangbusters. If you fail to include these points for the person you're reaching out to, expect to be ignored.

Here's an email Andrew sent that I've annotated to highlight the important parts:

SUBJECT: Steve Smith told me about you **[your subject line needs to grab the reader with your strongest hook, in this case a mutual connection]**

Hi Bob,

Hope you're doing awesome this Tuesday morning!

My good friend Steve Smith said you're his #1 pick of someone I should meet next.

Plus, I love your blog—especially the article on how to make it big in SF **[be detailed to elevate the compliment]**. I've been experimenting with Meetup.com events thanks to your inspiration. **[must be a truthful statement]**

Love to talk with you about how to do marketing for your business. **[your "gift"]**

How's next Tuesday at 10 am at Coupa cafe for you? Or whatever is most convenient for you. **[The more specific your call to action, the better]**

I'd also be happy to feature you in an upcoming blog post on my site, which has about 2,000 monthly readers. **[more value for the person]**

Thanks,
Andrew
P.S. About me: Just moved to SF, recently hung out with Marc Andreessen, Mitch Kapor, and more. **[social proof]**

> ## CHALLENGE
>
> ### Ask your friends for one referral.
>
> 1. Tell me the first person that comes to mind. Who's the most impressive friend you know?
>
> _____
>
> 2. Send this message to that friend:
>
> _____
>
> Hey <friend>
> You are the most impressive friend I know and I'd love your help in expanding my network.
>   I love: VR, 3D printers, email marketing.
>   Who's one person you think I should connect with?
> If no one comes to mind, no pressure.
>
> _____
>
> I like asking for just one person to make it easier to think about. And then say no pressure on the other person vs give them an assignment of having to introduce me to someone.
>
> 3. After you've had a great meeting with that person, thank your original friend and ask the new one for a referral.

You learned the power of starting now, you overcame your fear of asking, you figured out million-dollar opportunities and how to validate them quickly, you learned social for growth and email for profit, you mastered marketing, and then you learned how to figure out your dreams and accomplish them with amazing people. What's next?

Start Again

I remember visiting my father at his home in the last days of his life. It was a sad scene. Pill bottles and empty Sierra Nevada beer cans everywhere, my father drifting in and out of sleep on his La-Z-Boy chair as some crappy local news station played in the background. I sat next to him, staring glumly at the TV, feeling like a little boy again, yearning for his love and approval. I'd come to say goodbye, but I'd also come to tell him of my good fortune and thank him for the lessons that helped me get there.

As is my way, I tried to do it humorously: "No need to worry, Dad, I'm not here to crash on your couch. I got a place of my own now, and you won't believe it, but the business I started is actually going to do a few million in revenue this year. Amazing, right?"

"Yes, very nice Noah," he replied. "Can you change the channel please?"

That was it. No final father-and-son Hollywood scene. No wise words or weeping acknowledgment of how proud I had made him. Right then and there I could feel myself falling into a deep funk, insecurities rushing back, all those voices inside that no one can hear, that are always there and that we're never completely free from, growing louder and more insistent that I wasn't enough, that it would all come crumbling down sooner than later, and that Matt Cohler was right about me being a liability.

Crazy how our brains can flip on us, right?

I would have never imagined that day I got fired from Facebook over fifteen years ago would begin the adventure of a lifetime. I'm grateful they dumped me so I could go out and explore the world—my way. Today, I feel fortunate and excited that I can now share those lessons with you so you can create the path *you* want to live in *your* life.

The tests of your will and grit never stop. The doubts never quite disappear, no matter how much you achieve. A dying father might seem like a rare, dramatic example, but in moments large and small, **your life is shaped by your willingness to face your fears. Remember, just keep going no matter what.**

You have to define what success is for your life and not worry what others think. *Million Dollar Weekend* empowers you to create the life YOU want to live. And you get fifty-two chances to do it this year.

Achieving your dreams comes down to one question: How many times are you willing to get back up after falling down? Entrepreneurship is nothing more than the ability to come up with ideas and the courage to try them out.

To experiment, experiment, experiment. To fail, fail, fail. Until you succeed.

Just start. And then . . . start again.

Love,
Noah

PS: Shoot me an email, noah@MillionDollarWeekend.com. I'm here with you :)

MILLION DOLLAR WEEKEND
GRADUATE

CONGRATULATIONS TO:

_____

For completing the 48-hour challenge of
creating a business and changing your life!

Sincerely,

Noah Kagan

This page has been left intentionally blank
for your notes and inspirations . . .

Acknowledgments

- You are the first person I want to acknowledge. Well done on facing your fears, having a dream, and going after it.
- Tahl Raz. I dreamed for years of the chance to work with you on a book. Thank you for taking a chance on me. Somehow you were magically able to take all my adventures/theories/ideas/antics and put them together in a helpful narrative better than I could have ever dreamed. Thank you! Also for being a mutual lover of schvitzing.
- Adam Gilbert for our bike ride ten-plus years ago where I shared a dream to put my knowledge into a book for other people. And for always always always being my guardian angel.
- Chad Boyda for being a great partner and early advocate of this book.
- Neville Medhora for saving my ass in the last weeks to update the text.

- Maria Fernanda Salcedo Burgos for being you and taking care of me while I was writing.
- Lisa DiMona as my second mom and huge advocate the entire time of this book.
- Charlie Hoehn for being my secret weapon of writing and always reminding me to be Noah Kagan.
- Tommy Dixon for staying true to his beliefs and supporting me with the book launch.
- Nikki Poncsak for all the book research.
- Jeremy Mary for pushing me outside my comfort zone, creating great content together, and helping make amazing chapter titles for this book.
- Mitchell Cohen for a LOT of feedback on early versions of this book. And reminding me to always be more optimistic!
- Merry, Adrian, Stefanie, Mary Kate, and the team at Penguin for believing in the book.
- David Moldawer for helping put together the proposal that kicked this book off.
- Sam Parr for inspiring me to hustle.
- Ayman Al-Abdullah for inspiring me to be more consistent and always holding me to a high standard.
- Ilona Abramova for helping run AppSumo.com while I was working on the book and being great with sentences.
- Everyone at the AppSumo.com team!
- Thanks Cam Boakye (our YouTube editor) for helping create amazing content together and showing what an underdog can do.
- To every Sumo-ling and underdog out there who buys from AppSumo or enjoys my content—you inspire me when you go after your dreams.

- Dan Andrews (tropicalmba.com) for great bike rides and for being a business philosopher and great thinking partner.
- Tim Ferriss for providing the platform that helped make this book possible.
- James Clear, Vanessa Van Edwards, Ramit Sethi, Dan Martell, Mark Manson, Chris Guillebeau, and Ryan Moran for being available to share advice on how to write and promote a book.
- Every single person who left comments on the early drafts and was a part of the launch team. You know who you are.
- Peter Maldonado (chomps.com) for being the first person to instantly be down to support the book from his yummy company.
- My mom and dad for being my biggest advocates and teaching me so much.
- Throughout this book it made me realize HOW many people in our lives want us to succeed. I promise you have way more people than you expect who want to see you win. I'm one of them!
- If you feel that I missed you (my bad), insert your name here: _____

Notes

xix **Experiment-Based Marketing approach:** Noah Kagan, "Growth Marketing Mint.com from Zero to 1 Million Users," OkDork (blog), February 6, 2017, https://okdork.com/quant-based-marketing-for-pre-launch-start-ups.

Part 1. Start It

1 **There are two mistakes:** Note: This quote is widely attributed to Buddha; however, it does not originate from any known body of work.

11 **As my guy Ralph Waldo Emerson:** Note: This quote is widely attributed to both Ralph Waldo Emerson and Mark Twain; however, it does not originate from any known body of work.

Chapter 2. The Unlimited Upside of Asking

22 **Case in point:** Kyle MacDonald, "What If You Could Trade a Paperclip for a House?" Kyle MacDonald, TEDxVienna,

November 20, 2015, video, 13:22, https://youtube/8s3bdVxuFBs.

27 **When she was growing up:** Caroline Bankoff, "How Selling Fax Machines Helped Make Spanx Inventor Sara Blakely a Billionaire," The Vindicated, *New York,* October 31, 2016, https://nymag.com/vindicated/2016/10/how-selling-fax-machines-helped-sara-blakely-invent-spanx.html.

29 **if you initially get a no:** Daniel A. Newark, Francis J. Flynn, and Vanessa K. Bohns, "Once Bitten, Twice Shy: The Effect of a Past Refusal on Expectations of Future Compliance," *Social Psychological and Personality Science* 5, no. 2 (2014): 218–225, doi: 10.1177/1948550613490967.

Chapter 3. Finding Million-Dollar Ideas

42 **Steve Jobs said:** superapple4ever, "Apple's World Wide Developers Conference 1997 with Steve Jobs," YouTube, June 5, 2011, video, 1:11:10 [52:15–52:22], https://www.youtube.com/watch?v=GnO7D5UaDig.

42 **insists everyone at Amazon:** Amazon staff, "2016 Letter to Shareholders," About Amazon, April 17, 2017, https://www.aboutamazon.com/news/company-news/2016-letter-to-shareholders.

42 **The first of *his*:** "Leadership Principles," Amazon Jobs, https://www.amazon.jobs/content/en/our-workplace/leadership-principles.

52 **Mark Zuckerberg started Facebook:** Katharine A. Kaplan, "Facemash Creator Survives Ad Board," *The Harvard Crimson*, November 19, 2003, https://www.thecrimson.com/article/2003/11/19/facemash-creator-survives-ad-board-the/.

52 **And Microsoft started:** "Microsoft Fast Facts: 1975," Microsoft News, May 9, 2000, https://news.microsoft.com/2000/05/09/microsoft-fast-facts-1975/.

Chapter 4. The One-Minute Business Model

66 **Five minutes later:** Noah Kagan, "How I Made $1K in 24 Hours—Sumo Jerky," *OkDork* (blog), April 24, 2020, https://okdork.com/make-money-today/.

68 **his business Same Ole:** Christie Post, "Meet the New York City Dudes Who Will Wait in Line So You Don't Have To," The Penny Hoarder, August 13, 2020, https://www.thepennyhoarder.com/make-money/start-a-business/same-ole-line-dudes/.

68 **charging a $50 minimum:** "Pricing—Same Ole Line Dudes, LLC," Same Ole Line Dudes, accessed January 18, 2023, http://www.sameolelinedudes.com/pricing.

68 **and Robert himself:** Adam Gabbatt, "'A Five-Day Wait for $5,000': The Man Who Queues for the Uber-Rich," *The Guardian,* May 5, 2022, https://www.theguardian.com/us-news/2022/may/05/a-five-day-wait-for-5000-the-man-who-queues-for-the-uber-rich.

69 **Codie Sanchez has gained:** Kimberly Zhang, "Codie Sanchez: Builder of an 8-Figure Portfolio Buying 'Boring Businesses,'" Under30CEO, May 26, 2022, https://www.under30ceo.com/codie-sanchez-interview/.

Chapter 5. The 48-Hour Money Challenge

100 **Instagram started as:** Megan Garber, "Instagram Was First Called 'Burbn,'" *The Atlantic,* July 2, 2014, https://www.theatlantic.com/technology/archive/2014/07/instagram-used-to-be-called-brbn/373815/.

101 **Slack started as:** Kate Clark, "The Slack Origin Story," TechCrunch, May 30, 2019, https://techcrunch.com/2019/05/30/the-slack-origin-story/.

Chapter 6. Social Media Is for Growth . . .

109 **The only athlete:** David Adler and Manny Randhawa, "Tough to Choose: Top Two-Sport Athletes," MLB, February 1, 2023, https://www.mlb.com/news/list-of-top-athletes-to-play-2-or-more-sports-c215130098.

111 **marketing guru Seth Godin calls:** Seth Godin, "The Smallest Viable Audience," *Seth's Blog* (blog), May 22, 2022, https://seths.blog/2022/05/the-smallest-viable-audience/.

111 **or what *Wired* magazine:** Kevin Kelly, "1,000 True Fans," *The Technium* (blog), March 4, 2008, https://kk.org/thetechnium/1000-true-fans/.

112 **Take Danny Wang Design:** Danny Wang (@dannywangdesign), TikTok, accessed January 18, 2023, https://www.tiktok.com/@dannywangdesign.

114 **I had the luck to:** Noah Kagan, "How to Create an Email Newsletter," *OkDork* (blog), April 15, 2020, https://okdork.com/how-to-create-an-email-newsletter/.

117 **Justin Welsh has used:** "How Justin Welsh Built a $1,300,000 Business," Gumroad, November 21, 2021, https://gumroad.gumroad.com/p/how-justin-welsh-built-a-one-person-1-000-000-business.

117 **Former *Rolling Stone* writer:** Ross Barkan, "What Happened to Matt Taibbi?" *New York*, October 29, 2021, https://nymag.com/intelligencer/2021/10/what-happened-to-matt-taibbi.html.

117 **Nick Huber of The Sweaty Startup:** Nick Huber (@sweatystartup), "An update on my portfolio of businesses and an outline of my 5-10 year goals," Twitter, June 20, 2023, 10:26 a.m., https://twitter.com/sweatystartup/status/1671207958066212893.

117 **YouTube sub equals:** Jim Louderback, "Comparing TikTok, Instagram and YouTube Subscriber Value—Plus YouTube's 7 Year Itch and Much More!" LinkedIn, July 27, 2021,

https://www.linkedin.com/pulse/comparing-tiktok-instagram-youtube-subscriber-value-jim-louderback/.

118 **YouTube is the LARGEST:** Matteo Duò, "10 Best Video Hosting Solutions to Consider (Free vs Paid)," Kinsta, September 26, 2023, https://kinsta.com/blog/video-hosting/.

118 **It has 122 million:** Brian Dean, "How Many People Use YouTube in 2023? [New Data]," Backlink, accessed July 10, 2023, https://backlinko.com/youtube-users.

118 **massive like SunnyV2:** SunnyV2 (@SunnyV2), YouTube, accessed January 18, 2023, https://www.youtube.com/@SunnyV2.

121 **Ali is a massive star:** Ali Abdaal, "How Much Money I Make as a YouTuber (2021)," YouTube, December 16, 2021, video, https://www.youtube.com/watch?v=Toz7XEsSH_o.

122 **Dustin Wunderlich of Dustin's:** Dustin's Fish Tanks (@Dustinsfishtanks), YouTube, accessed January 18, 2023, https://www.youtube.com/@Dustinsfishtanks.

122 **he expanded to all things fish:** "DustinsFishtanks Profile and History," Datanyze, accessed January 18, 2023, https://www.datanyze.com/companies/dustinsfishtanks/397643365.

122 **Then there's Kyle Lasota:** Kylegotcamera (@Kylegotcamera), YouTube, accessed January 18, 2023, https://www.youtube.com/@Kylegotcamera.

122 **Andy Schneider, aka:** "All about the Chicken Whisperer," The Chicken Whisperer, accessed January 18, 2023, http://www.chickenwhisperer.com/all-about.html.

125 **An example of this is:** Matt's Off Road Recovery (@MattsOffRoadRecovery), YouTube, accessed January 18, 2023, https://www.youtube.com/@MattsOffRoadRecovery.

125 **Devin Stone of LegalEagle:** LegalEagle (@LegalEagle), YouTube, accessed January 18, 2023, https://www.youtube.com/@LegalEagle.

Chapter 7. . . . Email Is for Profit

128 **It started with a line:** Neville Medhora, "The Ten Thousand Dollar Day," *Copywriting Course Members Area* (blog), February 3, 2015, https://copywritingcourse.com/the-ten-thousand-dollar-day/.

134 **Remember the digital publisher:** Katie Canales, "Startup Founder Says He Lost His Company and $100 Million by Relying on Facebook: 'Sends Chills down My Spine' to Watch Others Build Businesses on Instagram and TikTok," Business Insider, February 25, 2022, https://www.businessinsider.com/facebook-startup-founder-littlethings-joe-speiser-2018-algorithm-change-2022-2.

136 **A healthy email list has:** "Email Marketing Statistics and Benchmarks by Industry," Mailchimp, accessed January 18, 2023, https://mailchimp.com/en-ca/resources/email-marketing-benchmarks/.

139 **On average, a person sends:** Jason Wise, "How Many Emails Does the Average Person Receive per Day in 2023?" EarthWeb, last updated May 13, 2023, https://earthweb.com/how-many-emails-does-the-average-person-receive-per-day/.

143 **YouTuber Nick True at Mapped Out Money:** Kayla Voigt, "How YouTuber Nick True Uses Dedicated Lead Magnets and Automations to Grow His Email List to Over 10,000 Subscribers," ConvertKit, March 22, 2022, https://convertkit.com/resources/blog/nick-true-case-study.

143 **Her superstar opt-in:** "The Story behind Love and London," Jessica Dante, accessed January 18, 2023, https://jessicadante.com/love-and-london.

148 **I happen to think:** Priscilla Tan, "The Best Paid and Free Autoresponder (How to Pick Yours in 15 Minutes)," Sumo, February 10, 2020, https://sumo.com/stories/free-autoresponder.

148 **I remember these guys commenting:** Leo Widrich, February 27, 2011 (10:22 a.m.), comment on Noah Kagan, "Daily Accountability Marketing Metrics," *OkDork* (blog), https://okdork.com/daily-accountability-marketing-metrics/.

148 **What I do know is:** Iyabo Oyawale, "How to Grow a Startup from $0 to $20 Million in ARR—The Buffer Story," CopyVista, January 11, 2021, https://copyvista.com/the-buffer-story/.

148 **To avoid fails like that:** Noah Kagan, "The SECRET to Becoming a PRODUCTIVITY MASTER (Never Be Lazy Again)," YouTube, August 12, 2020, video, 9:55 [02:56-04:58], https://www.youtube.com/watch?v=KLgIrxXvb44.

149 **Let me explain using a crazy:** James Clear, "Why Trying to Be Perfect Won't Help You Achieve Your Goals (And What Will)," *James Clear* (blog), February 4, 2020, https://jamesclear.com/repetitions. (Note: University of Florida professor Jerry Uelsmann shared his tactic with authors David Bayles and Ted Orland, who changed the subject from photography to ceramics in their 1993 book, *Art & Fear*. Clear's article offers an excellent explanation of both Uelsmann's tactic and the representation of it in *Art & Fear*.)

149 **This stops you from succumbing:** Seth Godin, *The Dip: A Little Book That Teaches You When to Quit (and When to Stick)* (New York: Portfolio, 2007).

Chapter 8. Growth

154 **in September 2007 :** Noah Kagan, "Growth Marketing Mint.com from Zero to 1 Million Users," *OkDork* (blog), February 6, 2017, https://okdork.com/quant-based-marketing-for-pre-launch-start-ups/.

159 **Daniel is a hobbyist climber:** Noah Kagan, "How to Create a $4,000 per Month Muse in 5 Days (Plus: How to Get Me as Your Mentor)," *Tim Ferriss* (blog), October 28, 2013,

https://tim.blog/2013/10/28/business-mentorship-and-muses/.

Chapter 9. 52 Chances This Year

198 **Harry has 100,000:** Marketing Examples, accessed January 19, 2023, https://marketingexamples.com/.

198 **30,000 LinkedIn followers:** "Harry Dry," LinkedIn, accessed January 19, 2023, https://www.linkedin.com/in/harrydry/.

198 **and 140,000 on Twitter:** Marketing Examples (@GoodMarketingHQ), Twitter, accessed January 19, 2023, https://twitter.com/goodmarketinghq.